D1376686

CHRISTMAS DAYS

ELF-LAND

CHRISTMAS DAYS

DEREK McCORMACK

POP

DESIGNED AND DECORATED BY SETH

ANANSI

Published in 2005 by
House of Anansi Press Inc.
110 Spadina Avenue, Suite 801
Toronto, ON, M5V 2K4
Tel. 416-363-4343
Fax 416-363-1017
www.anansi.ca

Distributed in Canada by
HarperCollins Canada Ltd.
1995 Markham Road
Scarborough, ON, M1B 5M8
Toll free tel. 1-800-387-0117

09 08 07 06 05   1 2 3 4 5

LIBRARY AND ARCHIVES CANADA CATALOGUING IN PUBLICATION DATA

McCormack, Derek
Christmas days / Derek McCormack ; illustrated by Seth.

ISBN 0-88784-193-7

1. Christmas — Economic aspects — Canada — History.
2. Christmas — Canada — History. I. Seth, 1962– II. Title.

GT4987.15.M328 2005   394.2663'0971   C2005-904102-1

Text design and typesetting: Brian Panhuyzen

Canada Council
for the Arts

Conseil des Arts
du Canada

ONTARIO ARTS COUNCIL
CONSEIL DES ARTS DE L'ONTARIO

*We acknowledge for their financial support of our publishing program
the Canada Council for the Arts, the Ontario Arts Council, and the Government of Canada
through the Book Publishing Industry Development Program (BPIDP).*

Printed and bound in Canada

CONTENTS

PREFACE

AN ADVENT CALENDAR for me. An Advent calendar for my sister. My mother taped them to the living room wall on November's final night. I remember the smell. Glue. I remember the snow. Glitter. It was made of metal. Snow was sharp.

Mom always bought the same kind of calendar: card stock printed with Christmas scenes — woods in winter, Santa's workshop, a Bavarian village by moonlight. Concealed in the scenes were numbers, one through twenty-four. Each number marked a window. Windows were hidden in fields, flowers, and clouds. A window could be in a tree.

Some kids got toys. A wooden animal a day. At the end of December, they'd amassed a menagerie. Some kids got candies. Their calendar windows concealed chocolates — chocolate turkeys, chocolate lambs. Mom always bought us the kind of calendar she'd grown up with. I popped open a window per day in December. Hidden behind? Images. Of objects — dolls, toy trains, candy canes. Things that make Christmas Christmas.

"The traditional kind," Mom called our calendars, meaning they'd been made in Germany, where Advent calendars were invented, and where most of the world's supply still comes from. I've never seen a Canadian Advent calendar. What, I wonder, would it look like? White, a sheet of white — a snowstorm. That's the scene I'd slap on the front. Glitter galore. As for the hidden objects, they'd need to be iconic, recognizable nationwide. What are the things that make Christmas Christmas in Canada?

1

FAKE SNOW

A WOMAN WALKS down Fifth Avenue in New York City. Christmas is coming. It's not here yet. The day's sunny. Warm.

Snowy. She's outside Lord & Taylor, the upscale department store. She stares at the show windows. In there, it's arctic. Snow is squalling. Mannequins wear winter coats.

The windows are the work of Dana O'Clare, Lord & Taylor's display director. In 1938, he blasted a soundtrack of storm winds out onto the sidewalk. "Blizzard windows," he called them, the first windows anywhere to combine sound effects and motion. O'Clare was twenty-five years old at the time. A show card in a blizzard window read: "It's coming — sooner or later."

Born and bred in Montreal, O'Clare's blizzard windows were a *succès de scandale*. The Fifth Avenue Association decried them, worried that motion in displays would "cheapen" the street. *Display World*, a trade magazine published by and for window trimmers, disagreed. It claimed that theatrical windows such as O'Clare's "made not only the store's customers conscious of display as a vital, interesting factor in selling merchandise, but the general public, the store's employees, and the trade."

O'Clare frosted his windows with a solution of beer and Epsom salt. A hidden hair dryer blew around barrels of bleached corn flakes.

Most Canadians made fake snow on a smaller scale.

"The effect of snow is easily obtained," said the Montreal *Gazette* in 1882, "and gives a very seasonable air to the decorations." *The Gazette* recommended glass flakes. Fragments of frosted glass, sold by stationers. Canadians sprinkled them onto Christmas trees.

Do-it-yourselfers made it themselves. "Pound roughly, or crush with a garden roller, any pieces of glass, such as old bottles, which have been saved up during the summer for this purpose."

Glass snow could cut. Hands. Paws. Cotton was safer, and cotton batting was cheap. In 1885, a factory in Marysville, Quebec, installed cutting-edge cotton-batting machines that spun out up to 200 pounds per day. *The Gazette* recommended tying tufts of cotton to the tops of tree branches, then teasing. "It must then be pulled out and made to look as light and natural as possible, hanging down in irregular points and masses over any projecting parts."

A magazine article suggested using jeweller's cotton. It was "thinner, easier to handle, and will split in the middle and not present that 'pressed-down' appearance." It cost more, but "about one-half the quantity will suffice, and the showing with this imitation snow makes the most brilliant appearance possible."

Decorators recommended cotton. Fire chiefs didn't.

"The tree should not be decorated with any inflammable material, such as paper, or cotton," said one safety expert. "Don't use cotton to represent snow."

Alternatives? Borax. Or ammonia. In the early 1900s, Canadian stores carried "Snowflake Powdered Ammonia" made in London, Ontario. It whitened trees, smelled strong.

"Glittering snow," said *The Halifax Herald*, "is produced by carefully scattering the tree ... with the thin shavings of powder of a tinner's shop." Another option was popcorn. "Each tiny sprig of the tree was tipped with a popcorn flake," wrote a Prairie reporter in 1907, "fastened on with a pin, and it took several papers of pins to 'snow-flake' this tree, but the effect repaid for the trouble."

Popcorn took patience. The impatient splashed trees with spirit gum, followed by fistfuls of flour.

I own an old Epsom salt tin. It's illustrated with a Christmas tree. "Epsom salt," the tin says, "increases stiffening properties of starch. And makes cheap artificial snow on Xmas trees."

Epsom salt does look like snow. Its crystals are prismatic, like snowflakes. They're needle-shaped, like some snowflakes. But they're uniform — no two unlike.

"Artificial snow on the topmost branches of the tree will add to its wintry appearance," said the *Manitoba Free Press* in 1903. It recommended mica, also known as diamond dust and as "Santa Claus snow."

Mica's a sort of salt. A silicate, really — salt and silicon mixed. In nature, it helps minerals form. It's lightweight, cheap, nonflammable, and safe, unless you breathe it. Mica dust scars lungs. Fibrous tumours form. Pneumoconiosis, it's called, or silicatosis. Coal miners get black lung. Mica miners get white lung. Snowmen, inside out.

"Don't put cotton under the tree to resemble snow," a fireman wrote in 1928, "nor on the tree itself. Use asbestos snow and mica." Asbestos snow was known as "snow drift." It looked freshly fallen. It was fireproof. Heat it up and it glowed Christmas-red.

"The uses to which asbestos has been put are many," said a newspaper article of 1908, "and new uses are daily found for it." Asbestos tape, cement, mill board, wicking, casketing. Asbestos insulated houses, pipes, and wires. Asbestos textiles went into firemen's clothing and fireproof gloves. Asbestos flooring deadened sound and discouraged vermin.

Mesothelioma — lung cancer caused by exposure to asbestos. It killed thousands of Canadians a year. Still does. No doctor diagnosed it until 1960.

I shake an antique snowdome. SOUVENIR OF CANADA. A polar bear's inside. It's ceramic. Snow squalls. Snowdome snow's known as "flitter." Plastic's the most popular flitter. Tinsel's used, too. This snowdome's old; it's full of antifreeze. The snow's made from bone chips, byproduct of abattoirs.

I light a cigarette. I don't smoke; this is an experiment. I'm testing a snowstorm tablet. "Snowstorm in a room," the package calls it. Comic books used to advertise snowstorm tablets. Irwin Toy sold them in Canada. I bought mine at a joke shop. I slip it into the business end of the cigarette. I take a drag. Nothing.

Then . . . *bam!* It ignites. White powder spurts. Another drag. My throat hurts. The powder's metaldehyde. A molluscicide, deadly to slugs.

I shake a can. Snow in a can, an aerosol. Instructions: "Decorate windows, wreaths, nativity scenes." Was there snow in the manger?

The warning label is a skeleton hand. DANGER. EXPLOSIVE. Canned snow's a chemical cocktail. Butane and propane keep the snow pressurized. Ethyl acetate keeps it soft.

This is the kind of snow I had as a kid. Stores sold it in "fluffy gleaming colours or white." It's made of stearic acid, from cows. Boil cow carcasses and jelly rises. It's crammed into cans, then perfumed. To smell snowy.

2

CHRISTMAS CRACKERS

THE QUÉBÉCOIS INVENTED tuques. Voyageurs and habitants knitted them from wool and fur. Tuques don't have brims. Tassels top them off. Each habitant family sewed their tuques with slightly different colours. The most common colour: red. Santa Claus's hat is a type of tuque.

Not all Christmas hats are so sensible.

"My guests were given sparkling headbands of silver tinsel with silver stars of different sizes fastened on the front end of them." So said a letter to *Party Magazine*, the Christmas 1928 number, published by the Dennison Manufacturing Company. *Party Magazine* printed instructions for crafting party caps from crepe. "A mat stock cone is the foundation" for a harlequin's cap. A flapper's cloche is red and white.

Dennison sold premade Christmas caps — dime per, dozen for a dollar — at novelty shops. In 1926, Toronto's Interlake Tissue Mills introduced crepe-paper party hats cut like jester caps, calpacs, tams. Nerlich & Company, a novelty company in Toronto, carried fezzes, majorette hats, jockey caps, "Indian Head Dresses," all cut from crepe.

No man made merrier millinery than Tom Smith. Tom Smith lived in London, England. He sold cake decorations — candy brides and grooms, spun-sugar roses that adorned wedding cakes.

He wasn't alone. Nineteenth-century London had plenty of wedding cake decoration salesmen. Smith needed a scoop, and Paris supplied it — the bonbon. A sugared almond wrapped in a twist of wax paper. England had no such thing. In 1847, Smith brought bonbons to Londoners as Christmas novelties. He sold out.

The following Christmas, he tucked mottoes into the wax-paper wrappings with the sweets. Romantic sayings. Poetic snippets. "Love proverbs," Smith dubbed them. The year after that, he decided to include charms, simple silver trinkets. Trouble was, they didn't fit in the twists. He put the charms and mottoes into tubes, then wrapped the tubes in pretty paper.

Tom Smith changed up his charms. Candles could be charms. Firecrackers, too. Smith invented snapper strips: stiff paper strips, the tip of each soldered to the tip of another with saltpetre. He concealed snapper strips in his tubes. Revellers yanked the twists apart. The saltpetre sparked. *Snap*. Loud, like a log in a holiday hearth.

Or such was the plan. It took trial and error. Too little saltpetre — no snap. Too much saltpetre — the strips smoked, burst into flames. Fingers burned. Everything burned. The tubes contained wax paper, tissue paper, crepe paper. Glued on top of the tubes were "scraps" — lithographed images of cherubs and Santa Clauses. Scraps, too, were combustible.

Smith called his tubes "Bangs of Expectation." Customers nicknamed them something else. In 1882, an ad in *The Morning Herald* in Halifax offered "Cossaques, In great variety." "Cossaques," it was said, echoed the crack of a Cossack soldier's whip.

Christmas crackers. That's what Canadians came to call them.

"We again beg to introduce Our Old Friend, Tom Smith, who has been dubbed THE KING OF CRACKERS." So went an ad for Fraser, Viger & Co., Ltd., of Montreal. The store carried Tom Smith Christmas crackers. In 1908, they advertised an array of styles, including:

* Holly Crackers
* Superstition Crackers
* Box of Puzzles Crackers
* Komikal Kamera Crackers
* Chinese Firework Crackers
* Cabinet of Curios Crackers
* Aldermanic Jewel Crackers
* Helitrope Red Box Crackers
* Sir Roger de Coverly Crackers
* Maypole Party (Perfumed) Crackers

Crackers contained bonbon-sized bottles of French perfume. Paste gems and scarf pins fell from Jewel Crackers. *Bang!* — bangles. Wedgwood china came in Wedgwood crackers. Some charms Smith imported from Germany; others, he made in his factory. Wax dolls that lay in crackers as if in coffins.

Romantic verses vanished, replaced by puzzles and posers. Tom's son Walter introduced contemporary quips. Maxims about wireless telegraphy and radios. "Aesthetic Crackers" included Oscar Wilde aphorisms. "Shakespearean Crackers" featured Shakespearean quotations.

In her 1949 memoir, Canadian artist Ruth Harvey recalled the Christmas cracker epigrams of her childhood. "I remember one that sounded as if it had been made up by some waggish don: 'Why is a misogynist like an epithalamium?' But most were better . . .'Why does a sculptor die a horrible death?' 'Because he makes faces and busts!'"

Crackers came in themed boxes. There were Golfing Crackers. Jazz Crackers. Crackers for spinsters contained miniature thimbles, night-caps, wedding rings, and faded paper flowers. In Bachelor Crackers, bachelors found pawn tickets, cigars, and decks of cards. For solitaire, I'm sure. Crackers for Married Couples held cradles, feeding irons, and frying pans.

Some Smith crackers contained the makings of masquerade parties. Paper masks resembling animals fell from Noah's Ark Crackers. From Character Crackers, Sarah Bernhardt and Prince of Wales masks. There were harlequin masks and Viking masks — "Carnival heads," Smith called them. Enchanted Crackers contained fake noses and eyebrows and eyes.

A father plays with his toddlers at the supper table. He's in a paper hat. It's striped. Devilish horns stick out the sides. The boy's cap is conical — a dunce cap — with candy-cane stripes. They appeared in a 1923 newspaper ad for digestive salts. A Christmas cracker sits beside a tray of sweets. My guess is it's a Tom Smith cracker. These hats are quality.

Tom Smith's caps, bonnets, and hats were designed by milliners, executed on millinery stands, better known as "blocks." His company used quality crepe. Plain and patterned. It produced fezzes for Turkish-themed crackers, Arabian headdresses for aspiring sheiks. King Tut headdresses for Tutmania maniacs. Shakespeare crackers boasted a series of hats worn by characters in the Bard's plays. Costlier crackers contained not just caps, but costumes. Patterned aprons cut from crepe.

As for "Sir Roger de Coverly Crackers," I have no idea what they contained.

Canadian stores stocked crackers from a variety of English suppliers. A Montreal shop sold Cracker Dolls — papier-mâché dolls in paper dresses. There was Baby Bunting, Phyllis Marie, Miss Rosie. Girls snapped them in half. Jewellery bled out. Morgan's of Montreal sold a selection of butterfly crackers, wings tipped in gilt. In "variegated colors such as yellow and petunia, green and tango, aero pink, green and red, green and primrose, blue and mauve." Eaton's sold Santas. Kids could shatter them to release the goodies inside. Kids pilfered "Santa's Mailbox," or snapped open a snow-covered schooner to get at its candy cargo.

Most popular of all were snowballs — papier-mâché balls containing all the gimcrackery found in Christmas crackers. Snowballs came in a range of sizes. Like in life. They came decorated with flowers. Unlike in life.

During World War II, German bombers blitzed the Tom Smith factory. Its library burned. Production slowed to a standstill.

A Victoria engineer started the Canadian Christmas Cracker Company. Fred V. Richardson had been concocting crackers for his kids for years with machinery he designed himself.

Richardson recognized the scarcity of crackers during wartime and started manufacturing crackers in quantity in his basement. In his first season, 1939, he made 500 boxes, a dozen crackers per box.

His crackers shipped across the Commonwealth. Grocery stores moved most of his merchandise. Richardson relocated to a small factory. He designed and built a machine for cutting and gluing paper caps. At full tilt, it produced 30,000 caps a day, in twenty different styles.

Wrapping paper, plastic prizes, cardboard tubes, mottoes — everything in Richardson's crackers came from Canada. The federal government issued him a permit to produce snappers. A drop of silver fulminate on one snapper; on the other, sand and glue. Pulling them apart effected "scratch detonation."

Since Tom Smith's day, snappers had been concealed. Partygoers pulled the ends of the wrapping paper and hoped that the snappers separated. Richardson changed that. He lengthened snappers. "The ends of the snapper are no longer lost in wrappings of paper," observed *Canadian Business* magazine, "but stand free and are easy to find."

"Crackers were part of growing up," says Martin Walpert. Walpert's father made paper products in Quebec. Paper plates. Paper cups. In the late 1950s, he introduced crackers. "My brothers and sisters and I ended up being the models for all the catalogues," Walpert says. "I have some old catalogues, from 1960. My family's got pictures of us sitting around the table with these stupid crackers going off."

Walpert remembers the toys their crackers contained. "They'd hang around the table a while; they always ended up in the buffet or sideboard drawer, guaranteed, until next Christmas. They'd sort of grow in that drawer, year after year, until Mom would throw them out."

Walpert's favourite toy? "A little tiny silver plastic cowboy. He had a moving arm. You'd position the arm behind the back of the cowboy, then flick it with his finger and he'd draw."

Does he still have it?

"Oh, God no, I don't still have it. It's funny . . . a lot of the gift items, the cheap novelty items that were in crackers then, are still used today."

Walpert's dad sold his business in 1965 to Perkins, the tissue-paper people. "Perkins wanted to build a partyware division. Dad went to work with Perkins to build this division. But, being a typical entrepreneur, he hated working for other people."

After Walpert Sr. resigned, he resuscitated his cracker concern. "I wouldn't have thought it was much more than 8,000 square feet," Walpert says, remembering his father's factory, which stood in downtown Montreal. "Basically an assembly line where the tube was rolled, the snap was put into it, the toy was put into it."

In the United Kingdom, cracker-making was, and is, a cottage industry, with outworkers finishing crackers at home. Walpert Sr. automated assembly. He designed and built a tying machine. "You took the cracker tube and you positioned it, and you put these two brass fittings on either end, and it worked on the basis of pneumatics. You pushed this button and air would wrap these cords around the ends, these specific tie areas, and crimp it. And you have a finished cracker."

Walpert struck up a relationship with Gordon Pennington, managing director of Tom Smith in England. Pennington had been instrumental in making Tom Smith the main cracker company in the world after World War II. In the 1960s, Tom Smith was shipping finished crackers to Canada. "The simple cost of the freight, because crackers were so voluminous, it didn't make a lot of sense." Pennington began to ship raw materials to Canada. Walpert assembled them and peddled them under the Tom Smith label.

Pennington left Tom Smith in the 1970s. Tom Smith cancelled its contract with Walpert, so Walpert went into business on his own.

The Canadian Christmas Cracker Company disappeared decades ago. Walpert Industries now dominates the Canadian cracker market. Martin Walpert's the president, succeeding his father, who passed on in 1992. Walpert *fils* maintains a Montreal office for sales. Production takes place in China. Walpert travels there twice a year to inspect output.

"People really don't quite grasp the level of detail and what's involved in the cracker business. If you're got a box of crackers with ten crackers in it, each cracker can have fifteen separate components." That means having an assembly line where every product has to be slightly different. "You want to be able to mathematically ensure that, as you're running these crackers through the machines, the toys are going to be different in the box."

Sometimes Walpert Industries designs its toys, sometimes it sources them out. Walpert crackers contain all types: jewellery, magnifying glasses, whistles, puzzles. Snaps he buys from Chinese companies. "All the snaps used to be made in England by a company called the

Reliance Snap Company. Problem was, they were really the only place in the whole world that you could get them, and when the demand for crackers grew in the 1980s, they couldn't keep up the supply.

"Meanwhile, there was a fellow in Korea who had started to build snaps. And his method of doing it was, rather than the paper wrap that's in the centre of a snap — a kraft-paper wrap that keeps the two sliding pieces together — he had plastic, which was shrunk over it. And so sometimes you could pull so hard, and these things would not pull apart. They were so tightly wrapped. And he went out of business. They were good snaps, man. They made a good bang."

And hats?

"Hats are all pretty much crowns. The shape or the profile could change. Colours change. It's almost always in tissue. We've done some different ones. We've done foil ones. We've done tartan."

3

TOY STOCKINGS

TOES CURL UPWARD, sleigh bells attached to the tips. Everyone knows what elves wear for footwear. Curly-toed slippers. For headwear, tuques with bells in lieu of tassels.

Rubie's Costume Company is among the world's largest makers of costumes. Headquartered in Queens, New York, the company has an office in Markham, Ontario. Rubie's sells elfwear. Tunics in harlequin diamonds, some in solids.

Rubie's also offers a slew of Santa suits in flannelette, velour, plush, deluxe plush, velveteen, Lyons velvet. Something called "Imperial Lux-Seal." For Mrs. Claus, there are aprons and mob hats. For Miss Santa, mini-skirts. I'm not sure who Miss Santa is. Mistress? Arctic ingenue? If Rubie's is to be believed, she's sexy. She wears velour sleevelets, fur capelet. Her neckline plunges. Legs sheathed in red fishnet stockings.

Fishnet stockings are not a Christmas tradition. Net stockings are.

"There were . . . starry tapers and glittering ornaments," wrote novelist Annie Fellows Johnston in 1901, describing a child's ideal Christmas tree, "with red-cheeked candy apples, and sugar animals hung by the neck; with tiny tarlatan stockings of bonbons, with festoons of snowy popcorn, and all that goes to make up the Christmas trees that are the dearest memories of childhood."

Tarlatan's a type of netting with a wide, square weave, giving tantalizing glimpses of sweets concealed within. Candy containers as ornaments. In the late 1800s, tarlatan stockings were common sights on Christmas trees. A Montreal newspaper referred to them as "the usual tarlatan bags."

Tarlatan: easy on the pocket, easy to find. Moms sewed stockings; tots emptied them. In the Maritimes, it was customary to give stockings to visiting friends.

In his book *Christmas in the West*, Hugh A. Dempsey reproduces a photo taken in 1917. A Prairie family's Christmas tree. Net stockings hang from the branches.

22

In the early twentieth century, cotton netting became as common as tarlatan. "White netting stitched in red or green shows off your effort and the gifts," said *Chatelaine*. Magazines recommended stockings sewn from silver netting, or red netting tied with tinsel cord. "If you lack a tree, string them along the fireplace."

"Special meetings were called to make the stiff net stockings," wrote a woman whose charity group threw Christmas parties for underprivileged kids. "Filling them is one of the happiest tasks." In 1928, underprivileged girls received a sample tin of cocoa, a large candy cane, a package of peanuts, a chocolate bar, a butterscotch bar, nuts.

"The Christmas Stocking," it was called. A novelty wholesaler named March Brothers advertised it in 1911. "This new and exceptionally unique device," the catalogue said, "is sure to delight the little folks beyond measure." The mass-produced version of Mom's tarlatan stocking cost $1.75 per hundred — "Made of woven fabric, similar to Tarlatan, but much stronger."

Commercial net stockings came in all sizes. The largest was the size of a boot. Smallest, a sockette. Some came decorated with pine cones or chromolithographed scraps or tiny bells. Stockings had strings to shut them. Hooks sewn in, for hanging on mantels.

Wholesalers sold net stockings to drugstores, candy stores. The stores filled them with sweets, then resold them for a pretty penny. Children swarmed department stores to see Santa Claus. Each child left His Eminence "bearing in triumph . . . a stocking stuffed with candy. . . ."

The *Manitoba Free Press* carried a story at Christmas 1904 on a city candy store called Boyd's: "The store is ablaze with light and gay with Santa Claus stockings, and there is no pleasanter place to sit down and watch the crowd."

Santa Claus Stocking was a trade name coined by Tom Smith, the Christmas cracker king. In the 1800s, he'd invent a new use for net stockings: stuffing them with toys. Small, medium, large, extra-large, jumbo; at the turn of the century, stores in Canada sold Smith's Santa Claus Stockings in five sizes. Jumbos were tall as tots.

Scarcely concealed beneath the red cotton netting were clockwork motor cars, clockwork railway trolleys. Those were for boys' stockings. In a girls' stocking, a girl might find a clockwork rocking horse, or a bisque baby. Some toys appealed to all. Metal mandolins and violins. Miniature grandfather clocks that chimed. Santa Claus stockings included games like Snakes and Ladders, Ludo, or card games with themes: Klondike Gold Rush, King Tut. There were flags and pennants. Santa Claus dolls. Boxes of chalk.

And fireworks. For indoors — "parlour" fireworks, as they were known. "To be ignited on a saucer or plate after the Christmas meal," according to a man who once worked for Tom Smith. Sparklers, exploding matches, Aspirin-like pills that exploded into sparks or snow at the touch of a match. A Tom Smith box from 1910 shows a girl shooting the star from a miniature Roman candle at a playmate across the parlour.

Mrs. Alice Howman started work for Tom Smith in 1935. "My job was to fill Christmas net stockings with little toys," she told writer Peter Kimpton. "My hands got red raw due to the roughness of the netting, and I didn't like it very much, as it was so repetitive."

Howman earned 37½ p per week. And ointment to soothe her skin.

In 1939, Morgan's Department Store in Montreal advertised Tom Smith Santa Claus Stockings "packed with books, toys, horns and other novelties youngers love." Shipments from Tom Smith stopped shortly afterward, as a result of the Second World War. Defoy and Legault filled the vacuum. Mendoze Defoy and Wilfrid Legault, Montreal wholesalers, offered their first toy stockings in the late 1920s, and sold several thousand.

"Before the war, our toy industry was small, strictly Canadian, and not too successful," *Canadian Business* reported in 1948. "The principal output comprised small metal toys, baby carriages, Christmas stockings, sleighs, wagons, dishes, and miniature skis." In those years, Defoy and Legault accounted for the bulk of the stocking business, importing toys from the United States, England, and Germany. In 1945, the company produced half a million toy stockings. Some stockings were mesh; some were fabric prints featuring snowmen and reindeer. Defoy and Legault sourced out Canadian suppliers. For example, Model Craft Hobbies of Toronto sold them hundreds of thousands of balsa airplane kits. At that time, Model Craft Hobbies was the largest model-aircraft maker in the British Empire. During the war, it had assisted the Canadian government in its investigations into wind-tunnel dynamics.

Defoy and Legault Stuffed Stockings shipped to stores across the Dominion. "Our biggest ambition is to export our line of stockings after this war," Defoy said. They'd already received one international order. From Newfoundland.

Still, some Canadians sewed their own net stockings. During the Second World War, women found fabrics hard to find, netting included. Stockings, said *Chatelaine*, could be crafted from "bits of mosquito netting, white or red, bits of leftover wools, a couple of snips with scissors and a few stitches with a large needle, you have this feminine-looking Christmas stocking ready to fill. And while talking of nets, try using huge bows of tarlatan in various gay colors for your boxes or other décor."

My mother grew up in Thunder Bay. Her parents always put a dollar or two in a neighbourhood Christmas pot. Money went to the milkman, who suited up as Santa and delivered toy stockings to all the children on his route. "They were the same toys you'd find in Christmas crackers," Mom remembers. Plastic dolls and pennywhistles. Dice. "They never lasted the day. But I loved them."

After the Second World War, plastic-netting stockings replaced cotton-netting stockings. Balsa, wind-up toys, fireworks — plastic toys replaced them all. In the United States, the Wannatoy Company specialized in plastic cars and trucks. Come Christmas, it'd pile up fifteen vehicles in a mesh stocking. Also available was a hollow plastic candy cane. Containing trucks.

"Packed with Profit!" promised a 1950 trade ad for Thomas Manufacturing of New Jersey. "Reserve your seat on the Thomas Christmas-Stocking Bandwagon of Profits." On offer: "2 Sizes for GIRLS — 2 Sizes for BOYS." In a small stocking — a foot and a half high — boys got a truck, a truck trailer, a battleship, a P-40 fighter plane, a Mexican donkey, a vinylite dog, and more. Small stockings contained ten plastic toys. Big stockings, sixteen. Slum — that's what the toys were called: a carnival word for the trinkets given away at midway games. Stockings themselves were red netting on the front, vinyl on the back. Nerlich & Company, the Toronto novelty distributor, offered toy stockings "WITHOUT PAPER STUFFING." Irwin Toy of Toronto carried a stocking "backed with cut-out game." It sold for a dollar.

Toy stockings still sell at dollar stores, manufactured by toy companies in China. Rubie's Costume Company sells empty net stockings. Churches buy them, stuff them for students in Sunday schools. Corporations buy them, to distribute at Christmas parties to the children of employees.

Some stores buy them in bulk so they can fill them with toys they haven't been able to unload. It seems unscrupulous. Stale sweets from Christmases and Halloweens gone by. An old candy cane that looks like a new candy cane. Kisses that could crack teeth.

4

DOLLS

THE QUINTUPLETS SIFTED through their stockings.

The Quintuplets pulled presents from beneath the Christmas tree.

The Quintuplets sat on Santa's knee. Someone snapped their picture. Santa was their doctor. Disguised in a mohair beard.

Christmas morning for the Dionne Quintuplets. It wasn't Christmas morning. It was November.

"There was no end to the demand for Quintuplet pictures," wrote Yvonne, one of the Quints. Yvonne, Cécile, Marie, Emilie, Annette. Born in 1934, their faces front-page news around the world.

The Newspaper Enterprise Association provided Quint pictures to the world — it held exclusive rights. Mr. Dionne, the Quints' dad, made the deal. He was forbidden, in fact, from photographing his own daughters.

"We celebrated every holiday from New Year's Day to New Year's Eve weeks in advance, so that the photographs could be sent out in good time to NEA customers," said Yvonne. "We poked our heads through cardboard Valentine hearts, carved pumpkins for Halloween, clambered happily on the knee of a Santa Claus. . . ."

The Dionnes of Callander, Ontario, already had five children before they had the Quints. The Quints didn't live with their family. They lived in a hospital a hundred yards from their home. The province of Ontario built it. The government owned the Quints. It took them from their family the year they were born. Mr. and Mrs. Dionne sued. It took them ten years to win back the girls.

Quintland. That's what the hospital compound was called. It included a parking lot. The public parked there, then shopped at souvenir shops. There were three, peddling pennants and posters and postcards. For a quarter, tourists could take pictures of an Indian living in a teepee. They snapped shots of a black bear caged in chicken wire.

Quintland closed for fall and winter. It was cold in Callander, near North Bay. It's not tundra, but it's close. Spring and summer, scores of tourists queued up at the observatory. A U-shaped building; on one side, a passageway, windowless. On the other, windows covered by a wire-mesh screen. The public peered into the playground where the Quints played in a sandbox, in a pool. Guards guarded them. Admission was free. Millions caught the girls.

Christmas days, Mrs. Dionne carted food and family to Quintland. Dr. Dafoe, ward of the Quints, greeted them. In 1935, Dr. Dafoe forbade the family from touching the Quints on Christmas Day. Lest the girls get germs. The Quints stayed behind glass. The family waved. In 1937, Dr. Dafoe relented and allowed the girls to dine with the family. He denied them turkey — too fatty. Chocolate, too, was taboo. In 1939, the Quints had woken early. Unstocked stockings. Nurses supervised. The Quints had telephoned Dr. Dafoe, wished him a *joyeux Noël*. The Quints welcomed their family mid-morning. The Quints sang carols, beat on drums. A wire report: "The family all seemed to enjoy the Christmas party."

At Christmas, the Quints got gifts galore from their family. Their mother made them something special every yule. Mittens, maybe, or muffs. Mufflers. Gifts arrived from their doctor, from nurses, from policemen, firemen and teachers. The parish priest. The public sent dresses and bonnets, blankets and booties. Coats and coat hangers.

And dolls. "Dolls of all descriptions," according to the Canadian Press.

"Her Most Treasured Possession" is how a Canadian department store described a girl's doll. Doll-Town. Dollyland. Palace of Dolls. Department stores constructed elaborate display areas for their holiday dolls. Smaller stores improvised, hung dolls from clotheslines.

A department store in Montreal transformed its auditorium into the Toyville Opera House for Christmas 1922. Every hour a "Beauty Chorus of Darling Dollies" climbed onstage and sang "Tell Mother I'll Be There." Hands hidden under the stage made them move.

Some stores installed doll hospitals. A shopgirl in a Red Cross nurse's costume greeted girls. She'd show shoppers "the 'surgeons' hard at work putting in glass eyes, attaching heads, arms and legs. . . ."

Inuit have made dolls for millennia. Long before Canada was Canada. Dolls carved from walrus tusks, from whalebone. Bone arms and legs attached with string or sinew or gut. Dolls carved from wood, anatomically correct. Hair came courtesy of sled dogs — moulted fur woven into wigs. Inuit girls made their own dolls. In doing so, they learned how to sew, how to cure fur, how to fashion clothing from cured fur.

Ojibwa crafted dolls from spruce roots, or skins stuffed with spruce moss. The moss decayed. So did the skin. Iroquois crafted dolls with cornhusk bodies, dried apple faces. Animals ate them. Early Plains Indians tied leather about buffalo hair or grass. Something soft.

Tribes on the Pacific coast made dolls of cloth and leather. Inside them, cavities to contain quantities of tea. Dolls full of tea smelled much better than dolls full of moss.

Some indigenous peoples sold their dolls to northern settlers and to collectors of Native art. Many settlers made their own dolls, or bought dolls at dry-goods stores. By Confederation, Toronto dry-goods dealers were offering dolls from a couple of countries. From *Puppenland* — "Puppet land," part of the Black Forest of Germany — came dolls with papier-mâché heads. France shipped dolls with wax heads. Wax dolls are difficult to keep. Years yellow the skin, which cracks in cold. In heat, the wax doll melts. Soot and dust stick to it. As do flies.

Rag dolls came from America. Machines cut bodies from muslin. Seamstresses stitched them together, then stuffed them with cotton wool or sawdust or bran. Girls painted faces — piecemeal work. Girls sewed garments, silk petticoats and stockings, lace jabots. Girls who could never afford silk petticoats for themselves.

The Dominion Toy Manufacturing Company Ltd. opened its Toronto factory in 1911. Dominion started off making stuffed animals, teddy bears. It later experimented with "composition." A German invention, composition was a mix of glue, sawdust, and corn starch. "When thrown forcibly against a brick wall [the dolls] drop to the ground without the slightest dint or injury."

Eaton's hired Dominion to make Eaton Beauties. It turned out to be a plum contract. Eaton's Beauty doll sold oodles. As doll historians Evelyn Robson Strahlendorf and Judy Tomlinson Ross once put it, "To own an Eaton's Beauty was the desire of almost every little girl in the Dominion of Canada."

Dominion was Canada's first successful doll company. Then the Reliable Toy Company bought Dominion, becoming Canada's biggest doll company — the Commonwealth's biggest doll company. Reliable consumed most of the cornstarch made in Canada. Cornstarch and pine dust, kneaded in containers as water and rosin were added. It came out as a kind of dough. Workmen pressed the dough into moulds, baked it. Furnaces fired, workmen "stripped to the waist," according to *Maclean's*. What came out of the ovens? Half legs, half heads, half torsos. Gluers glued them together. Sanders sanded down seams. The limbs were dipped in lacquer.

Dolls visited beauticians. Doll heads, anyway. Heads propped on pikes, women workers painting on eyebrows and lips with permanent paint. Rouged cheeks applied with blowguns. How much rouge was right? Until the dolls had "the hectic flush of a confirmed consumptive on each cheek," as a Prairie newspaper put it.

Women workers inserted glass eyes into sockets. Cheap dolls had hair painted on. Fancy models got wigs. Hairdressers permed curls, or curled hair with irons. The hair, mohair — the wool of angora goats. Mohair holds its colour and its curl. It is stronger than human hair. Some dolls received caracul wigs. Caracul, shaved from the skin of very young Asiatic or Russian sheep. Caracul was slippery. The wigs slid around the skull, slid off. Unless stapled down.

Reliable's factory included a knitting mill. Seamstresses sewed smocks, stockings, and shoes. Some dolls, the expensive ones, were dressed in satin and lace. Cheap dolls were dressed in cotton. A shop in Reliable's factory manufactured miniature shoes. Another shop turned out voice boxes, little phonographs that could be surgically inserted into dolls. Adults made the recordings. "Mama," they said. "Papa," they said. "I'm sad." Some dolls cried real tears, or made real water, after girls filled them with water. The water wore down the composition. Dolls decomposed.

"There are literally hundreds of Reliable composition baby dolls out there in various stages of decomposition and disrepair," Sheila Callen says. "I get them all." Callen's into dolls. She mends them. The name of a business she runs in Langley, British Columbia: A Timeless Doll Hospital.

"I do minor touch-up things, such as new eyelashes and broken toes to the ones that have cracked-open heads. Chewed-off feet. Matted and dirty mohair wigs, rotten cloth bodies. They all come home looking like they just came out of the box.

"Something about recreating our childhood," she explains.

"I had a Baby Wettums doll," she remembers. "I made clothes for her by taking scraps of fabric and cutting holes in the top for her head and hand-stitching the side seams. They were beautiful."

Callen grew up in the 1940s. "My family was extremely poor and had very little. Christmas was a simple occasion, but we always had a tree with decorations and gifts under it. Most gifts were handmade in secret. I had very few dolls." Sheila coddled Baby Wettums.

"When I was six, I wanted a baby carriage for my doll and was hoping for a beautiful one like one of my friends had. When I woke in the morning and found a very small, all-metal, simple-looking carriage, I was heartbroken."

As an adult, Callen packed away her dolls and became a middle manager in municipal government in British Columbia. "A captive employee," is the way she put it to me. In 1991, she stumbled across a dollmaking class. "It was possible to make one's own porcelain dolls," she says. "I was smitten." She signed up and sculpted a doll. When it was done, she didn't sleep. "I sat on the edge of my bed until 1 a.m. looking, touching, holding my doll. Crying a lot."

Callen made more dolls. Her dolls won her blue ribbons at shows, earned her a Certified Master Doll Artisan diploma. With honours. Callen left her job and began crafting dolls — from porcelain, plastic, composition — in her garage, which she converted into a studio. "It's heated, ventilated. A delightful place to work. It was not like work. I had died and gone to heaven!"

Callen now teaches dollmaking. "I started teaching classes with one student, which grew to a total of four full classes a week. It was phenomenal!"

She conducts her classes in her workshop, and sells her dolls at fairs. "A large portion of my business is at Christmas. Mothers want to give dolls to their girls. Girls want to give dolls to their mothers. I'm exhausted."

Christmas is mad. "A few years ago I decided to branch out into porcelain Christmas tree ornaments." She makes Santas, angels, gingerbread men. Snow babies — reproductions of ornaments popular at the turn of the last century. "We do not recommend snow babies be given to children as toys," reads Callen's catalogue. "Also, the sparkles could be harmful if swallowed in large quantity, and we've all seen children sucking on things unnatural!"

For Callen, Christmas fairs are social affairs. "I get a chance to dress up a bit and meet people. I come up with my own creations and test the market. Instead of always repairing and restoring dolls."

"I get many Barbara Ann Scott dolls," Callen says of her restoration work. Barbara Ann Scott was a figure skater, a gold medallist for Canada at the 1948 Olympics. An American designed her doll. Reliable produced it. Sold it by the sleighful.

"I had one myself," Callen says, "and when I chanced upon the opportunity to buy an identical one, I thought I had died and gone to heaven. They're very special collector dolls to Canadian girls. As are Shirley Temple dolls, of course."

"The Shirley Temple doll is still the freak of the industry," reported *Maclean's* in 1938. Despite the Depression, Temple dolls sold by the million in Canada. "Roguish, merry-eyed Shirley in miniature," said an ad for Morgan's of Montreal. The Temple doll had more than fifty different costumes. Each Dionne Quintuplet owned a Shirley Temple doll.

Dionne Quintuplet dolls — they're scarcer. According to a *Maclean's* article, they "never went over to any degree in Canada." The first Dionne dolls appeared in 1934. The family licensed the rights to an American firm, Madame Alexander of New York. When Madame Alexander shipped the dolls to Canada, the government taxed them — at 60 percent duty. The price became prohibitive. A single Dionne cost three dollars — six times as much as Shirley. And no child wanted just one. Madame Alexander sold sets of five dolls, in boxes, in baskets. Cuddled up together in a crib. The dolls were identical. Colours distinguished them: Yvonne wore pink, Marie blue, Cécile green, Annette yellow, Emilie orchid. The girls had jointed limbs. Heads turned. Eyes shut when the dolls laid down. Sleep eyes, they're called. Stamped on their torsos: Madame Alexander.

Canadian girls didn't want for Dionne-abilia. There were Dionne calendars, lithographed by Rolph Clark Stone in Toronto. There were tablecloths, tableware, souvenir spoons, souvenir cups. Colouring books and postcard books. Yearbooks: *Dionnes at Two*, *Soon We Will Be Three!*

Canadian girls kept Dionne scrapbooks. At Christmas, they struck gold. Papers ran pictures of the Quints playing with dolls. With their doctor. The Quints building a snowman. With their doctor. The Quints colouring Christmas cards to mail to the King and Queen. As one paper put it: "Quints are the King's legal ward."

In 1940, Canadian newspapers ran a comic strip, *The Quints' Christmas*, starting in December, with the Quints holed up in their hospital playroom.

"Remember, Nurse said if you wish for something, all you have to do is keep on wishing and wishing and you'll get your wish!" says Marie. In reality, Marie was the smallest Quint. In the comic, all Quints looked the same. Monogrammed smocks distinguished them.

What do the Quints wish for? Escape. To Toyland. A doll appears to them, named Hello. He's see-through. In his belly are the cogs and boxes that keep him running. Hello whisks the girls away on clouds. The Quints meet the moon.

"Help! Help!" exclaims a Quint. "The world is burning!"

"Don't be frightened," says Hello. "It is just the sun coming up to say, 'Hello!' to his friend, Hello!"

In Toyland, the Quints meet Mother Goose. Humpty Dumpty. The Big Good Wolf. Santa, they tell the girls, is on strike. He's refusing to make toys for a world full of tyrants. Like Hitler. The Quints will try to persuade Santa to return. Mother Goose wishes them luck.

"We," says Cécile.

"Thank," says Marie.

"You," says Emilie.

"Mother," Yvonne says.

"Goose," Annette says.

5

PARADES

THE TEDDY BEAR was born in 1902. Stuffed bear dolls had been around for a decade before that, made by German and British companies. "Stuffed bears," they were called.

Then came President Theodore Roosevelt, nicknamed Teddy. Roosevelt hunted bears. In Louisiana, he treated an injured bear kindly. By killing it.

A Brooklyn firm started selling teddy bears through Butler Brothers, a distributor that specialized in toys. Butler Brothers shipped the teddy bears to Canada, where Wilfrid Laurier was prime minister.

There were no Laurier dolls.

Canadians tried to come up with an animal doll to call their own. W. J. Philips taught art at a high school in Winnipeg. He drew an owl. Billy Owlet. Billy appeared in a children's book.

Billy Owlet wore white trousers, a red waistcoat, and a green tie. A pale blue topcoat. A newspaper in England described him thusly: "There is a cocksure look in his eyes and a devil-may-care aggressiveness in his yellow hooked nose."

Billy Owlet was big in England, as an illustration and as a doll. Queen Mary bought a Billy Owlet doll for her daughter, Princess Mary. A regal endorsement. Stores sold out. It was Europe's most popular toy for Christmas 1913. Canada had scant supplies.

"This toy," said the *Manitoba Free Press*, "is expected to supplant the 'Teddy Bear' in both England and Germany." The paper quoted a British toy store manager: "For many years, inventors have been trying to find a successor to the teddy bear, but the only toys that seriously challenged his supremacy were Fi Fi and Tubby, a comic cat and dog."

In Canada, a hundred small companies made stuffed animals. The workers: women who sewed at home. A cottage industry. A newspaper article from the 1940s reported that some Canadian stuffed animals were filled with "inedible" material, toxic to children. Some were stuffed with dirt. In one case, investigators found a doll full of undisclosed "vermin."

Eaton's didn't take any chances. It hired Merrythought, an English toy firm, to produce Punkinhead, the store mascot. Created in the 1940s by an artist who worked on Eaton's Christmas catalogues, Punkinhead was a brown bear with a knot of blond hair atop his head. Merrythought made Punkinhead from plush mohair. He was stuffed with something septic. Cotton swabs? A tag stitched to Punkinhead read, "Hygienic Toys."

Eaton's introduced Punkinhead at Christmastime 1948. Besides dolls, Eaton's sold Punkinhead tea sets, mittens, and sweatshirts. Eaton's bakeries served Punkinhead cookies. Ginger. Every kid who saw Santa at Eaton's got a Punkinhead story book and "a gift of candy." Punkinhead had his own song, "Punkinhead (The Little Bear)." Country-and-western star Wilf Carter recorded it on his Christmas album.

Punkinhead also starred in the store's largest annual promotional event: The Santa Claus parade.

Santa rode a train to Toronto's Union Station. The Grand Trunk Railway delivered him. It was 1905. The first Santa Claus parade. Santa ate eggs and bacon at a diner, then hopped into a horse-drawn truck. His seat: a packing crate painted red and black. He heighed the horses onto Front Street.

Children waited on the sidewalk. Santa waved, tossing candy and nuts. He steered up to Eaton's Yonge Street store, took off his costume, returned to work. Santa was an employee picked from personnel. The horses went back to delivering parcels.

That same year, Santa telegraphed the *Manitoba Free Press*: "My reindeer are in the pink of condition, my travelling arrangements are complete, and if all goes well, I hope to arrive in your city about Saturday."

The message appeared in an Eaton's ad. A few days later, it ran another ad: "Nothing of great interest has happened since my deer were drowned." The reindeer, Santa said, fell through ice in northern Manitoba. "I am truly lonesome without my reindeer."

A train delivered him to Winnipeg. From the station, he took a tally-ho drawn by a team of drays. A lone trumpeter heralded him. Santa threw candy bars to children. The manager of the Eaton's store stood beside him. He, too, threw candy bars. Santa couldn't throw fast enough.

A train ride to a station, a carriage ride to a store. This is how Eaton's structured its earliest Santa Claus parades in Winnipeg and Toronto. Montreal didn't get an Eaton's parade until 1925.

Which isn't to say Montreal didn't have Christmas parades. In 1907, Santa's train pulled into Montreal's Windsor Station. He mounted an automobile filled with teddy bears. The auto wound up Peel Street to the store of G. A. Holland & Son.

In 1913, Santa Claus climbed into a biplane in Cartierville, Quebec. The plane climbed over Mount Royal. Saturday afternoon, thousands staring from the streets. The biplane alit at Fletcher's Field. Assistants escorted Santa to an automobile. He hobbled, frostbitten. It took ten minutes to warm him up.

Santa, announced ads for a Montreal department store, would fly into the city in a hot-air balloon. Santa, announced ads for another store, would fly in a dirigible.

"Our Santa Claus," read an ad from 1910, "has got hold of a flock of cockatoos to bring him in his carriage to Montreal." The illustration showed an army of cockatoos reined to a sleigh. "He says that the birds are the best kind of flying machines ever invented." The ads were mostly stunts. Stores got press for Santa processions they never had to stage. Santa never flew into Montreal in a dirigible, never flew in a cockatoo-powered sleigh. Though that store did install a sleigh in its Santaland, with cockatoos tied to it. The cockatoos sang songs.

Peter the Pumpkin Eater, Cinderella, Goldilocks, Miss Muffet, the Cow that Jumps Over the Moon. By the end of World War II, Eaton's parades starred a slew of fairy-tale figures in costumes sewn by store seamstresses.

Costumes consumed thousands of yards of fabric every Christmas. Satins, mostly. Striped satin, polka-dotted satin, satin in harlequin diamonds. For Punkinhead, a fake-fur jumpsuit.

Employees played parade extras. Parade organizers sent word to high schools. Needed: size 10 clowns, size 6 elves. Parade morning, students assembled at public schools. Seamstresses darted around, pinching, pleating, altering with safety pins. Men wore tights, as did women. Tights are classic elfwear.

Beauticians from Eaton's cosmetics counters greasepainted paraders. Some paraders wore wigs. Some wore heads sculpted from foam and papier-mâché — pig heads, wolf heads. Papier-mâché was lightweight, until it got wet with rain or snow. Then, according to Eaton's historian Patricia Phenix, "the comical, oversized heads became too heavy to balance on parade participants' shoulders, causing those wearing them to bob and weave dangerously into the crowds."

An Eaton's employee told Phenix, "You'd see people holding what was left of their heads, charging through the crowds."

"We still have a walrus head," says Martha Miller, a costume director for Toronto's Santa Claus parade. "It's almost as old as the parade." A century. "It's around here somewhere."

She's searching for the walrus head in parade headquarters, a warehouse in an industrial park. Hundreds of heads are mounted on walls, like hunting trophies. Bunnies. Clowns. Who hunts clowns? "I'm not sure what happened to it," Miller says. "It should be in a museum."

Racks of costumes run along walls. Miller's not sure how many costumes there are. Thousands. "We have everything," she says. "You want a bug, there are bugs. You want an elephant, there are elephants." She works full time, year round, sewing, mending, altering. She can make a butterfly into a caterpillar. "My favourite costume is an orange monkey. It's maybe fifteen years old. Bright orange. It's a costume you wear because you want to be noticed." She shows me a princess's dress. Navy lamé. "It still looks great on the street." She turns it inside out. The lining's yellowing. "It's about thirty years old. We still use it."

"We make new costumes, too," Miller says. "I think last year we made about 150 costumes. I get ideas from different places. I might notice something on television, or in a film." I notice a bookshelf. Volume upon volume of fairy tales. Miller's working on a new costume — the Diva Fish, she calls it. "It has a long tail that drags on the ground. It's kind of funny."

"I'm from Windsor," Martha Miller says. "Well, not Windsor — nobody knows where Thamesville is. Robertson Davies was born there." Thamesville puts on its own Santa Claus parade. "My parents are actively involved in it every year. They own a hardware store, so they put a float in it every year. I was on a float five or six times," she says. The float was a flatbed drawn by a Ford tractor. Miller's father drove.

"The float was for Girl Guides. We sang Christmas carols at the top of our lungs. We weren't really characters. We wore winter coats. It was freezing."

Miller studied fashion design at Seneca College in Toronto. "I thought I would probably move to New York and work right beside Donna Karan. I'd just show up and she'd let me work. Why not?" She laughs.

"Even when I was in school, my projects were theatrical things. They said to make a skirt, so I made one of black outlining and painted it with fabric paint. My teacher suggested I try out for a job that was listed on the wall at school."

Had she ever seen the parade?

"On TV," Miller says. "I've never seen it live. The morning of the parade I'm at the school trying to get everyone into their costumes. So I've never seen it. When I leave here, I'll see it."

Miller started with the Santa Claus parade in 1998. "Ann Frederick-David does as much stuff as I do," she says. Miller and Frederick-David work side by side, at antique sewing machines. "She's an amazing sewer. I can sew, but I'm not as great as her. I do more of the administrative stuff."

People who want to march in the parade have to fill out an application form. "Standard stuff: their name, their age, their address. And then they also have to measure themselves. They measure their chest, their waist, their hips. The length of their arms, their head circumference. They write down if they wear glasses or not."

The costumes are cut large. Paraders can fit a sweatshirt or sweater beneath them. "The costumes aren't warm," Miller explains. "Once people get walking they start to sweat. Adrenaline kicks in." There's a washing machine at the parade's headquarters. It cleans a costume per load. "Mr. Clean works really well. It's really hard on your clothes, but we only wash things once a year." What about moths? "Knock on wood, we haven't had a moth problem. Moths go for things like silk and wool. We don't use anything that isn't polyester."

Christmas parade floats first appeared in the 1910s. Winnipeg's Eaton's parade of 1919 featured eight. Workhorses drew a slab of Swiss cheese with mice, "big as children," gnawing at it. A huge duck bobbed its head while fairies rode it. Fairies pranced about a giant mushroom. Floats carried a jazz band "making the jolliest kind of noise." A "funny band featuring acrobats." The marching band had to march.

Carpenters employed by Eaton's built the floats from lath and wood in a warehouse on the banks of the Red River. Work began in summer. "This is when the parade is designed and the color scheme chosen," read one Eaton's ad.

In fall, the store set up an assembly line. Silhouettes of figures were sketched on paper. "The shape is then cut in wood, modelled on a trailer, padded with wire, excelsior and cotton. . . ." Painters painted the wood with poster paint in primary colours. In the 1940s, fluorescent paint made its debut.

The warehouse was unheated. Work got cold in winter. After the parade, the men busted up floats for scrap. What wasn't useful — crepe paper and fabric and wood oddments — was burned. Which warmed the workers somewhat.

Nearly fifty floats floated by in Toronto's 1955 parade. Eaton's in Toronto employed ten full-time parade workers. Artists and sculptors designed floats. Carpenters constructed them. Students from the Ontario College of Art did the decorating. They got a bit of money, and academic credit. They used up fifty pounds of bronze powder, and 100 pounds of glitter, per parade. Paperhangers hung hundreds of rolls of foil paper on floats. Foil paper sparkled, even on dull days. Eaton's stuck signs on its floats: *Jack Spratt*, *Humpty Dumpty*. "Since many parents aren't up on their nursery rhymes," explained Jack Brockie, the parade's organizer.

Floats moved forward along the five-mile route, winding up in a warehouse. Workers stripped them down. Started again from scratch. "When space ships and supermen come in, I go out," said Brockie. He preferred storybook standards, with one exception. A Punkinhead float. Kids loved it. Kids waited for it. Kids in Punkinhead sweaters. Punkinhead mittens clapped.

"I always believed that Christmas never started until it had snowed and until the Santa Claus parade had come," Murray Pay says. "Then you knew that you were going to get your presents."

Murray Pay was a kid in Winnipeg in the 1940s. Come Christmas, he'd travel downtown to see the Eaton's Santa Claus parade. See the Christmas windows at Eaton's, and sit on Santa Claus's knee. In his twenties, Murray Pay went to work at Eaton's.

"Eaton's had a year-round facility in Winnipeg that produced their floats and costumes to get ready to do the Santa Claus parade. I rebuilt floats, or redecorated and repainted last year's floats. We tore a couple apart each year and rebuilt them. And I worked at it all night. The Eaton's philosophy was, there was a magic to Christmas."

Pay did a stint in the Eaton's store, too, helping to build Santa's castle in Toyland. "Kids lined up and went into a maze. Some kids went one way, some kids went the other way. They all went into the same castle. And saw Santa. But there were two Santas in the same castle. A wall between them. So the kids never saw the two together."

Pay moved to Calgary, where he worked as a display man in department stores. His first year there, he judged floats in the Calgary Stampede's youth parade.

" I looked at some of the crap that was being judged, and I said, 'I think I better go at it.'" Pay had a float in the Stampede parade the following year. "It was built the night before. I pre-built props at home, put it all on a semi-trailer, put it through the parade."

He won. "The next year, we went pro." Pay worked as a freelance float-maker. "We did the float for Holiday Inn. We did Sears. We developed a reputation. We travelled to Oktoberfest in Kitchener. We've been to the Montreal Grey Cup . . . Vancouver, down into the Pacific Northwest of the United States. We competed. We won."

When Pay says "we," he means himself, his wife, Elaine, and his crew: the Floatbusters. They designed floats, constructed them, taught workshops on design and construction. "A float's a story on wheels, floating on a sea of asphalt," he says. "The float's a pop-up book. It's a story that takes you into a magical world of fantasy. When you look at a Santa Claus float, the magic goes from beginning to end. Anybody playing music in the parade — are they going to be playing some classical piece? Some march piece? They're going to be playing 'Jingle Bells.' And, of course, Santa Claus is at the back of the pack, ready to go. So many people think it's cute to put him up in a fire engine. But for heaven's sake, he rides on a sleigh with eight reindeer. Maybe Rudolph. Maybe."

Murray Pay literally wrote the book on Canadian parading: *On Parade! The Organizer's Guide to Planning Parades and Floats*. It's the only book of its kind ever published in this country. He co-wrote it with Barbara Kwasny. "My thoughts are one thing; to put them into proper language is another," he explains. Kwasny put them into proper language.

"Build safe," Pay says over and over. Floats are fraught with hazards. They're flammable, covered with dyed cotton and crepe. "I was the very first company in Alberta to insure a parade float," Pay says. "First to put fire extinguishers on floats." Floats need waterproofing, too. As a magazine article once noted, rain, sleet or snow "could play havoc with the glitter."

Tractors pull floats — sometimes. Sometimes floats conceal cars. Drivers peer from a small window cut from the front of the float. No rearview, no peripheral vision. Workers must make sure engines are tuned; a stalled float stalls the whole parade. And fumes must have a means of escape, or drivers could suffocate. "Is someone parading near an exhaust pipe?" Pay says. "Does that exhaust pipe get hot?"

Don't build floats too big, Pay says. Underpasses demolish them. Low branches will knock Santa Claus down. Men and women often have to sit inside float figures, pulling levers and pulleys that make heads bob and eyes roll and tongues loll. Frostbite's also a worry. "There's a lot of stupid things we do in parades," Pay says. "Maybe that's what you should put in your book: the stupid things we do in parades."

Eaton's cancelled Winnipeg's Christmas parade in 1967. Winnipeggers were moving out of downtown, escaping to suburbs. They got sick of standing in the street, freezing. They watched the Toronto parade on television instead.

In 1968, a bomb exploded in the basement of Eaton's Montreal store. The FLQ put it there. The Front de Libération du Québec. A militant separatist organization. The following day, Montreal police discovered dynamite connected to a clock concealed in Eaton's jewellery department. Police evacuated the premises on Friday afternoon, the eve of the Christmas parade.

Eaton's boarded up show windows. Bomb squads sniffed out the store. The chief of police couldn't guarantee the safety of the public. The parade went ahead as planned, but for the final time. Montreal's Eaton's store cancelled it permanently. In 1969, Montrealers watched Toronto's parade telecast.

In 1996, Eaton's went under. Stores shut down. The Toronto Santa Claus parade is sponsored nowadays by a host of corporations and retail stores.

"We have a ball of yarn that was donated," Martha Miller says, "when Eaton's got rid of their yarn. There's actually one that says, 'Punkinhead Approved.'"

Miller had never heard of Punkinhead. "Since then, I've seen a lot of Punkinhead merchandise popping up in antique shops." He fell from favour in the 1970s and was soon forgotten. Even Miller doesn't think much of him. "The spelling — is it a pumpkin? Isn't a pumpkin more Halloween? For me, I always go right to the food. When I hear 'Punkin,' I think pumpkin pie."

I ask if he's still around, in spirit, in costume.

"There's nothing here," Miller says. "I bet the heads have been destroyed. The brown, fun-fur jumpsuits are now something else. Monkeys, maybe. Or chipmunks. Paint stripes up the back, it's a chipmunk."

6

SANTA CLAUS

I'M IN A mall. "Silent Night" plays. On loudspeakers. I walk past Zellers. I walk past Canadian Tire. I'm a dot on the mall directory. I could be at any mall anywhere, but I'm in the east end of Montreal.

"You need help?" asks the lady in the information booth.

I shake my head. History happened here.

"I'm on a pilgrimage," I say.

In 1899, this wasn't a mall. It was Fairyland. "Sweet music will make the place like a beautiful fairy-land," said an ad in the Montreal *Gazette*. "The store is literally packed to ceiling with Xmas Presents. In the evening a brilliant illumination of colored electric lights takes place. Don't miss us to-day for a genuine treat."

A department store, G. A. Holland & Son, took out the ad. It once occupied this space. Santa Claus stalked the aisles, stood in the show window. The first department-store Santa in Montreal.

By 1900, rival department stores had installed their own Santa Clauses. "Santa Claus . . . is now in FAIRYLAND at OGILVYS, ready to receive the little ones." Ogilvy's Santa Claus exhibited "Beautiful Pictures of all the Wild Animals he has met in his travels." Lions, tigers, elephants. Santa handed each kid a box of candies.

Holland updated Santa's show. Santa was surrounded with soldiers from the South African contingent, Canadian infantrymen who'd battled in the Boer War. Santa entertained "all with thrilling accounts of his experiences in 20 of the engagements." The store staged the fun in a reception hall alongside a display of firearms and ammunition. Admission was a nickel for children, a dime for adults. Store rules: "Perfect order maintained. No crowding allowed."

A trade magazine called him "The All-Important Santa." "No matter what else the toy buyer does in the way of an additional attraction for the little fellows, unless they see a sure enough alive Kris Kringle cavorting around among the toys, cutting up jolly capers, receiving and answering letters, giving inexpensive presents now and then, the holiday toy display is not quite complete."

Stores needed Santas, scouted them through theatrical agencies. Ageing actors, veterans of the vaudeville circuit, out-of-work clowns, out-of-season carnies.

In 1905, the Santa at G. A. Holland & Son staged a dog-and-pony show, "To show what kindness will do in the animal kingdom, and how human many dumb creatures are."

"Entrance of the smallest dog pony in the world." That was the first act. Then a bear played banjo, a bear waltzed with a dog, a bear juggled a ball while a dog stood atop it. A monkey raced a dog. A dog and a bear teeter-tottered.

"In addition to the bears there are: 2 large German Poodle Dogs, 2 French Poodle Dogs, 1 Russian Poodle Dog, 1 English Whippet Dog, 1 Fox Terrier, 1 Coach Dog, 1 Rhesus Monkey, 1 South American Ant-Eater." The anteater ate ants.

"It had always been a good stunt to put Santa Claus in the street window for at least part of the day," observed a trade magazine in 1909. In cities across Canada, Santa climbed into display windows at set times.

Windows were dressed to look like living rooms. Santa seemed to step out of a chimney. Santa sat at his desk. Making a list.

At another Canadian store, Santa was joined in the show window by three kids of kindergarten age. The kids tinkered with toys. Santa then "demonstrated for their benefit the workings of the different mechanical playthings — a demonstration which was watched with considerable interest by the throngs outside the window."

A business magazine recommended that Santas stay in windows for not more than an hour or two at a time. Windows offered Santa little legroom. Why did Santa flee the show window? He got Claustrophobic. Windows got hot. Footlights blazed, burned to the touch. Frost formed inside. Window dressers drilled holes through the glass, letting arctic air inside. Through it all, Santa would sit there, in furs, shivering.

Eaton's outdid all. Up until the end of the First World War, it staged Santa spectaculars in theatres. In Toronto, it rented Massey Hall, distributed thousands of tickets for free. In Winnipeg, the show went on at Walker Theatre. "The stage had been transformed into a cave of wondrous beauty." Crystal stalagtites depended. Monster seashells doubled as scenery. Princess Curly Locks starred in a play "into which there were cunningly woven the favourite nursery rhyme characters,

Mother Goose, See-Saw Marjorie Daw, Simple Simon, Jack and Jill, Little Jack Horner; a good harlequin, a clown, 10 green-clad gnomes who had wicked designs on the princess, six Charlie Chaplins in costume, 10 Maypole dancing fairies, 10 policemen in blue uniforms . . . the soldiers of France, Italy, Russia, and Britain in uniform."

As the play concluded, white reindeer drew Santa onstage in a chariot. He sang patriotic songs. "Rule Britannia!" "God Save the King."

Clowns and carnies cussed and drank. Cigarettes yellowed their beards and teeth. If they had teeth. During the Depression, Charles Howard played Santa Claus on the toy floor of a department store in upstate New York. Howard hated sloppy Santas. Hated their speech — their *dese* and *dem* and *dose*. Hated their wild ways. In carny slang, "reindeer dust" is cocaine. He condemned the Santas as "unqualified for their jobs, spiritually and physically." He decided to teach them a lesson.

In 1937, Howard sent a letter to department stores across America. "Does your Santa know the right answers to all the questions asked? Can he advise parents about the proper toy for each child? Is he a salesman, a showman, a student of children? Santa Claus means more than red pants. We know your store expects more, and you know the public expects more."

Howard established the Charles Howard Santa Claus School in Albion, New York. The term: one week. Tuition was fifteen dollars. Classes commenced with the singing of "Jingle Bells." Curriculum: "What parents expect of Santa; how toys are made; child psychology; showmanship and salesmanship; and children's Santa stories." Students graduated with a B.Sc. — Bachelor of Santa Claus.

In Howard's day, an unschooled Santa earned ten or fifteen dollars a week. A graduate of the Santa Claus School made up to five times as much. Santas signed up for membership in the National Association of Professional Santa Clauses. In 1938, the association's president echoed Howard. "I believe that we should make this profession a tried and strict one," he said, "not allowing just anyone to come into it unless duly qualified by manner of speech, character and general appearance."

The association safeguarded the interests of Santas, protesting stores that didn't hire Santas, decrying window displays that featured Disney characters — Donald Duck and Mickey Mouse — in lieu of Saint Nick. They won concessions for their members — smoke breaks, shorter shifts. They held a convention in 1937. On the agenda was determining what the standard length of a Santa Claus beard should be.

"The beard should not be so long," the association argued, "that it will get tangled up in the gears of electric trains; nor should it be so short that it will not convince young skeptics."

Stores didn't have to hire Santas.

A "lifelike figure of the venerable dispenser of Christmas toys and candies" stood in the show window of People's store in Halifax in 1882. A western stationer displayed a Santa doll in his show window in 1924. "He was surrounded by jointed dolls, who had their arms outstretched to him. The effect was that of tiny children begging for presents."

Butler Brothers, a mail-order house headquartered in Chicago, made automated dolls. Santa Claus with clockwork insides. Simpson's installed them in toy departments in the 1940s. "See and Hear Simpson's Laughing Animated Santa Claus." A "huge Santa Claus" stood in the window of the Simpson's store in Montreal. "He is an animated Santa Claus and he laughs and chuckles and slaps his knees, showing the greatest good will to everybody." Not everybody showed good will to Santa. Hugh MacLennan once decried an animated Santa who sat "in the window of department stores in a cheap red suit, stringy whiskers and a mask which is a caricature of a face, and for a month before every Christmas he laughs continually with a vulgar roar."

Canada's priciest Santa? Birks' diamond department built him. Santa's coat consisted of rubies. Diamonds doubled as fur trim. A tuque of rubies trimmed with emeralds and pearls and lined with sapphires. Birks' Santa stood eight inches tall. He cost $30,000. He wasn't for sale. He appeared in Birks stores in 1920 to stimulate sales.

In the 1930s, he was dismembered. Made into bracelets.

In 1959, a professional Santa named Henri Paquet established *l'Association des Pères-Noël*, or the Quebec Association of Santa Clauses. The association supplied Santas — live Santas — to department stores. When department stores died out, Santas moved into shopping malls.

"Shopping centres, that's around 140 or 150 hours in December," said Eddie Martin, the association's president. A reporter from CBC Radio interviewed him in 1963. "They get a couple of breaks in the morning, and in the afternoon, but they have to work until six or seven o'clock.

"We got around 200 people working for us at Christmastime," said Eddie Martin. "We try to locate the big fellow and he learns how to do Santa Claus. They have to mix with the children and they have to like the children. They have to weigh around 250, and have height around six, six one."

The association still employs a couple of hundred Santa Clauses. Most work part-time. Santas and Mrs. Clauses. The association supplies them with suits and beards. Or dresses.

Second-hand suits aren't enough, says Santa Victor in his book, *All About Being Santa: The Manual of Bringing Joy*. "Better costuming translates into a better bottom line." The book forms the syllabus of Santa Victor's Santa School.

"Santa Victor" is the stage name of Victor Nevada, professional Santa. He plays the part at shopping malls, parties, and parades, all over western Canada. He hails from Calgary. He's starred in commercials for car companies.

Santa Victor started playing the part in the 1970s. "My initial performances were poor," he says. He studied, steeped himself in Santa lore, Santa songs, Santa literature. "I talked to as many Santas as I could find." He signed up for a Santa school. "I found it lacking," he says. So he founded his own school in 1997. Class is conducted in conference centres or banquet halls — whichever his pupils prefer. Santa Victor is willing to travel. "Most people think all you have to do is put on a Santa suit, practise your ho-hos, and you're ready to go," he says. "Nothing could be further from the truth."

A session of Santa school lasts a weekend. The curriculum consists of a series of study units, including Toy Knowledge and Paradability. In the Business unit, Santa Victor teaches invoicing and bookkeeping, "so Santas get a good grounding on how to succeed in their market areas." In How to Pose for Photographs, students learn to "create a happy feeling inside." This feeling gives photographs "that sparkle that Santa should have." In the Makeup/Wigs & Beards unit, students study "selection, cleaning, and maintenance." Each student receives a makeup kit with cosmetics for eyes, lips, and cheeks. The History & Philosophy section asks, "Who is Santa? Is he an elf or a human being?"

7

SANTA SUITS

At Christmas, my parents pull out a picture. Me, sitting on Santa's knee. Bawling. Santa's skinny. His suit's saggy and orange. It wasn't machine washable. He machine-washed it. The photo's from a department store in my hometown. I was five years old. I believed this man was Santa Claus. Now I think, Santa was a hack.

If only it had been Santa Victor. Santa Victor has a slew of Santa suits. In his closet: a red coat, ornamented with gold braid and scores of antique brass buttons. Vintage black-patent buckled shoes with Cuban heels. Stockings striped with candy-cane colours.

Santa Victor designs all his clothes. Has seamstresses sew them. It's Christmas couture. Yves Santa Laurent.

In old Europe, St. Nicholas was a religious figure, the patron saint of children. And pawnbrokers. And perfumers. A skinny, stern saint in long robes and mitres.

But not in North America. Canadians knew St. Nick from a poem, "An Account of a Visit from St. Nicholas," which Clement Clarke Moore wrote in 1822. Moore made him jolly, jelly-bellied, more elf than man. "He was dressed all in fur from his head to his foot and his clothes were all tarnished with ashes and soot."

What kind of fur was it? What colour? Where did he get it cleaned? Moore didn't say. An 1837 painting depicts a scene from the poem. Santa's short, sinister. In a fur cape, brown pants and a navy-striped jacket.

The look never caught on.

In 1863, during the American Civil War, Santa got a makeover courtesy of Thomas Nast, an illustrator for *Harper's* magazine. One illustration has him dressed in garments borrowed from Uncle Sam: a fur-trimmed, star-spangled coat with striped trousers.

When war ended, Nast put Santa in fur Union suits. They came in brown, black, and green. Santa wore them skin-tight, accessorized with patent pilgrim shoes. A tasselled hat. Holly sprays. It was Nast who first depicted Santa residing in a palace at the North Pole. An

1866 *Harper's* illustration shows Santa spying on children with a telescope. His palace is made of snow and ice, ideal for storing furs.

"Thomas Nast was an observer of Parry and Franklin and other early polar explorers," Santa Victor explains. Franklin died in the Arctic in 1847. Parry, in Germany, in 1855. "Perhaps that's where he got that look."

Santa Victor wears red velveteen. Fun-fur furbelows. For now. "I use fun furs ranging from short to medium to long shag," he says. "Perhaps real fur will become acceptable again, and when it does, I'll use that."

Santa in furs.

Santa in short pants and argyle socks.

Santa in a tam, a capelet on his back.

Santa in a black oilskin coat with a black floppy hat.

I'm looking through ads in the Montreal *Gazette*. Old issues from the end of the nineteenth century. Santa's depicted in a slew of styles.

Among the ads, an ensemble stands out: a suit with fur trim, black boots, and a broad, black belt about the belly. Belt buckle big as a photo frame. Who created this suit? Who knows. But it cropped up frequently across Canada and the United States. In catalogues, on greeting cards. In colour cuts, the suit was scarlet. It became ubiquitous. "The orthodox costume," a newspaper called it.

So why did the red suit stick? Cultural critic Karal Ann Marling calls it a "highly decorated business suit." It appealed, she argues, to an American sense that Santa was a businessman, an entrepreneur overseeing a successful toy factory. I don't know if that's true. What I do know is that Santa's a winter. Scarlet suits his complexion.

"The early department-store Santas took their costumes out of tickle trunks," says Santa Victor, "or what the store had lying around for them to wear. Ads and promotions in the early days were usually local in nature, and as such there was no standard look. That's why perhaps you see a wide range of outfits, from fur coats to tuxedos. It took Coca-Cola's international marketing campaign in the early 1930s to give everyone a standard Santa look."

Haddon Sundblom drew Santa for Coke. Santa, to Sundblom's mind, was a big man — big, broad, and burly. "I prefer the look of Norman Rockwell's Santa," Santa Victor says. "He's an elf, not a human. It's more true to who I think Santa is."

By the late nineteenth century, Canadians were dressing up as Santa. Surprising their kids, amusing church groups. Most men didn't own scarlet suits. They put on togas — swaths of red felt or muslin tied at the waist. Boots were bolts of black oilcloth wrapped around shins. Any trousers would do.

Some Santas wore red bathrobes. Some wore whatever. "We heard a great noise, and the boys, they said it was old Santa Claus come," said a Blackfoot boy in a letter to the *Calgary Herald* in 1894, "and we all ran out and there he was coming over from the Mission house with a long white beard, and a dress like an old woman, and a bundle of things on his arm and we all laughed at him. . . ."

"To make a Santa Claus costume is quite easy, inexpensive and creates endless fun," wrote Mrs. E. F. Ashby in *Farm and Ranch Review* in 1928. Mrs. Ashby lived near Edmonton. She recommended buying red flannel, white buttons, and scarlet thread. All other costume components, she said, "may be had for the making."

The coat: Mrs. Ashby patterned hers on a man's dressing gown. She cut it large, so it could be stuffed with pillows or worn by men of varying widths. The tuque she stitched from scraps. Ditto the stockings.

"On our farms are wild rabbits which are now turning white," she wrote. A Santa suit required seven skins, fat and meat removed. Preferably tanned. "Trim off the ragged edges (the tail and legs) and with a sharp knife carefully cut the skin into a long strip." Strips adorned cuffs and cap. A single skin was used for a collar.

In 1915, a Prairie newspaper printed a recipe for readers: a simple solution of alum and water. The solution wasn't pricey, wasn't poisonous. It fireproofed fabric. "The use of this solution is a safety measure which should be employed for pageants, carnivals, and receptions . . . and as a safeguard at all amateur Christmastide and New Year displays."

The alternative could be agonizing. In 1905, a teenager in Victoria dressed up as Santa for her high-school holiday pageant. Her robe grazed a candle. Students stampeded. It took her teacher minutes to smother Santa's suit. In 1929, a union of travelling salesmen sponsored a pageant for Winnipeg children. Santa lit a smoke while waiting to go onstage. His beard caught fire. Fire spread to the suit. Flannel burned fast, fur trimmings took some time. Spectators tore off the costume. Santa was sent to hospital having suffered burns to his face, legs, arms, torso, and hands. He survived. Scarred.

According to Santa Victor, the first professional Santa suits became available in the 1930s. "Charles Howard was the first department store Santa," he says. Howard had trouble buying quality Santa suits, so he started the Santa Claus Suit & Equipment Company. The first firm to specialize in Santa suits. Red velvet with real rabbit furbelows. He sold them to students of his Santa school. He sold them to Macy's. Santas sported them during Macy's annual Thanksgiving Day Parade.

"Some of those suits still survive," Santa Victor says. Santa Victor relishes comparisons between himself and Howard. Like Howard, he makes expensive suits. Expensive, but enduring. Like Howard, he sells accessories — spectacles, with or without prescriptions; double-stitched toy sacks; hand-stitched stomach pads. Shabby Santas stuffed pillows in their coats. The swankiest suits had inflatable rubber stomachs sewn into them.

Christmas 1932. A Santa stopped by a Halifax school to distribute toys and candy to students. A lad of fifteen latched onto Santa's beard. Tugged. Santa "smote the youth lustily upon the ear," according to the Halifax police. They arrested Santa for assault.

Santas need beards. But beards are trouble. Kids swing from them. Kids stick candy in them. "Beware of the dog!" said a professional Santa in 1925. "A red costume and long whiskers are an invitation to trouble if a good sporty dog gets a look at you."

Nineteenth-century Santas spirit-gummed cotton to their jaws. Cotton balls, wool, strands stolen from mops. In an early Norman Rockwell illustration, Santa's trying on a store-bought beard — a muslin base with clumps of cotton attached. Dime stores sold them. Cigarettes ignited them.

Santa masks sold everywhere — department stores, street vendors at city markets. Some were papier-mâché. Most were made from stiff cloth covered with wax and paint. The wax absorbed smoke, sweat, soot. Wax yellowed, paint flecked, hair came unglued. Some masks had painted-on whiskers. Some had cotton wool glued on.

Mrs. E. F. Ashby made her own mask.

"[Dad's] chin and cheeks are covered with a piece of brown paper," she wrote, "over which is drawn a piece of cloth on the bias and fastened on top of the head." She glued hair to the chin — hair scissored from the mane of the family's "old grey mare." For a moustache, she trimmed white fur from her collie. "Holes are cut for the ears," she wrote. "A piece of garter elastic is sewn on the top to securely hold it in place."

Santa had better not be allergic to animals. Or afraid of ticks.

I visit Malabar Ltd., a theatrical costume house in Toronto. Malabar's almost a century old. An early catalogue featured a Santa Claus mask, made of buckram, for ten cents. Santa masks died out in the 1950s, when Santas started creating looks with cosmetics. Pan-Cake powder. In 1958, *Maclean's* magazine described Santa as "that incredible mountain of flannel, fur, moth balls, hair and red grease paint."

Angora beards appeared during the Depression. As did yak hair beards. Yak hair's the gold standard of Santa beards. As soft and white as snow. Moths devour it. Depending on length and weight, beards can cost hundreds. Some Santas ordered German-made beards woven from human hair. The beards tended to be short. Long human hair's rare.

Mary Beley made wigs for Simpson's display department. For Santa, she made beards. "Though Santa sits . . . in our Queen St. window," she told the Simpson's employee newsletter in 1945, "his whiskers still get pretty grimy. It's one of my jobs to keep them white and fluffy so a luxing and marcel is in order." In the 1950s, Toronto's health commissioner worried that Santas might be sick with colds, flus, or something worse: tuberculosis. Beards had to be disinfected daily with soap and hot water.

The Second World War introduced synthetics. Nylon beards could come in any length. They were slow to burn, and washable. The thing is, synthetic hair doesn't look like human hair. It looks like clown hair. And the bottom of the beard barrel? Even worse than synthetic beards, according to *Weekend Magazine* in 1977, were "the crummy-looking cotton [beards] which are not really suitable for Santa."

Malabar still sells Santa suits. Made in China. Robes of velveteen. There's the Deluxe, the Super, the Supreme. One size fits all. If the suit's too big, stuff it. There are Santa sets — wig, beard, moustache combos — made in Quebec. The hair's "Kanekalon," a word not found in my dictionary. Chin cups hold beards in place; wires, moustaches. The beard on the most expensive set is extra long and extra wide. It lies like tuxedo ruffles on the chest.

Santa Victor sports a real beard styled with gels and waxes. "Maybe even some glitter, depending on my mood." He painted it white. He didn't like it. Now he bleaches it — "for authenticity," he says. "Hairdressers say it can't be done, or raise horror stories about the process. Trust me, it can be done, you just have to find the right person."

Good grooming doesn't end with a beard. "Refrain from eating strong-smelling foods such as garlic" is a tip Santa Victor teaches amateurs. Another yule rule: "Outgrowths of nasal hair will not be tolerated."

"Everyone who plays Santa for a period of years and is serious about developing the character should come to an ever-deeper understanding of who Santa is," Santa Victor says. "I don't play Santa the same way that I did when I started. Hopefully, my characterization of Claus has gotten deeper and more subtle over the years."

His character has changed. So have his costumes. "Clients love the different looks I give them. The children connect with me as the 'real Santa' because I'm the only Santa they see dressed differently." Santa Victor's devised his new look. Gone is the tuque. "The hat used for this season will be a red three-corner hat," he says. There'll be no fur on his jacket. Sleeves will be rolled up. "I plan on eliminating the red colour in my costume. It'll be interesting to see what happens."

8

SANTALANDS

I'M SHOPPING FOR a castle.

"This is the last one I did," says Eric Field. Field designs castles. He's showing me his catalogue. The castle's carved from ice and snow. Styrofoam ice. Styrofoam snow. It's painted in polar hues — white, silver, aqua — and it stands at a story and a half. "The latest in North Pole accommodations," the catalogue says.

"I wanted to do something with fantasy," Field explains. Icicles accessorize the castle. Sold separately: a Christmas tree covered in icicles; toy soldiers, icicles hanging like epaulets from their shoulders. A pair of polar bears. They glitter. They're made of mesh with glitter glued on.

"Sold," I say.

Field laughs. I'm a writer. The castle and its accoutrements cost big bucks. Where would I erect it, anyway? In my kitchen? The castle's what display artists call a "Santa setting," what was once known as a "Santaland." It's designed for shopping malls. Santa sits inside. Kids visit. The polar bears look pretty.

"Children," asked an old newspaper ad, "did you ever see Santa Claus' home?" It should have said Santa Claus's homes. Store display staff designed them, carpenters executed them. In different years, Santa had different digs.

In 1904, Eaton's stuck Santa in a booth. He stood behind a counter, dolls tacked to a wall behind him. Another year, the store stuck Santa on an ark. It resembled a houseboat afloat on a blue tarp. Kids crossed a gangplank to see him. Santa's cargo: a pair of every type of animal. Stuffed animals.

In the winter of 1911, Goodwin's was one of Montreal's premier department stores. It contained a cave — an "ice cave high up on a mountain top." In truth, a storeroom painted blue and white and hung with tinsel icicles. Santa's home away from home. Fairies ushered children in to meet him, then ushered them out. Salesgirls, I presume, played fairies. "This year," a newspaper reported, "fairies are dressing yellow and pink."

"Santa lives away in the frozen North, in a huge cave on the side of a snow-capped mountain." So read a 1914 ad for Eaton's in Winnipeg. Santa sent Eaton's a cable: Build a cave for me, and I'll come stay there.

Eaton's carpenters constructed a plaster cave. Kids whispered wants to Santa and to his plush toy pets. "Santa lives right among the bears, the lynx, and lots of other fierce wild animals," the ad said. "He thought you would like to see them." The animals sat on straw. A lion that paced and roared when wound up. A bobble-headed polar bear.

"How about caves?" I ask Eric Field. "Still popular?"

"We've never made a cave," he says. Field is the chief designer at Display Arts of Toronto. Display Arts' clients include malls, bank towers, and sports stadiums, department stores having largely died out. "We do a lot of custom designs. Everyone wants exclusivity." Field once designed an igloo. Santa sat inside; kids crawled in.

"Where was that built?" I ask.

"It was never built," he says. No one ordered it.

Some years, Santa went upscale. David Spencer Ltd., a Vancouver department store, built him a house in the 1920s: a cottage of plaster and dark beams in the Tudor style. Very Beatrix Potter. Santa sat in his yard. A polar bear ushered children to him. Another polar bear guarded the mailbox where children posted letters to Santa. A third played in the spruce trees about the house. Not polar bears so much as men in polar bear outfits. Santa's beard was cut from the same cloth as the snow on the roof. The sky? The department store's ceiling. Water pipes ran across it. Lamps hung low.

Eaton's Winnipeg store did something similar. "I have sent word that I want a house built in Toyland just like the one I live in here," Santa said in an ad. Period photos show a cabin built with rough-hewn planks. There was a porch where Santa sat. Elves sat with him, riding hobbyhorses. "Also a stable for my deer and a post office for my letters," Santa said. Santa's reindeer were real. They endured a week in the store. A week of petting, poking. The store smelled like droppings. And like candy canes.

Display Arts offers a Country Christmas Santa Setting. "Something distinctly Canadian," as the catalogue puts it. A wood cabin. A wood fence. "That's a real split-rail fence," Field says. "And the twigs are real." A twig wreath on the door. In the yard stands a reindeer made from fire logs. Trees look like jack pines. They're made of lath and canvas. "We spray it all with fire retardant first," Field says.

"A castle's a fantasy," Field says. "A safe haven." It's also the standard shape of Santa settings. Display Arts of Toronto sells a castle of toys. Santa sits on a throne, in the shadows of super-sized Christmas stockings. "We use light material," Field says, "so nothing will fall."

In the 1950s, Eaton's stores put up Toyland Palaces. Toy soldiers guarded Santa. A scene stolen from *Babes in Toyland*, the 1903 play, in which toy soldiers serve a Toymaker. Whom they ultimately murder.

"The gingerbread's Styrofoam," Field says of a candyland Santa setting he created. A gingerbread castle in which a giant gingerbread man guards Santa Claus. Field tested this setting on his own children. They tore through it while he watched for anything they could tear down.

Candyland evokes *The Nutcracker*. Clara and the Nutcracker Prince journey to a Land of Sweets. The palace garden's spun from sugar. "Hansel and Gretel" is another touchstone. In 1946, Simpson's in Toronto erected a "sugar candy castle." In candy colours. Built from lath and wood. As a kid, I visited a shopping mall that had a spectacular Santaland. A gingerbread castle caulked with frosting. A foamcore fairy tale, fatal if eaten. It stood in a food court.

The Franklin Expedition. The Parry Expedition.

The Kleinschmidt Expedition. Not nearly as notorious. In 1936, the

Winnipeg Free Press ran a series of accounts by Captain Kleinschmidt of his cross-Arctic trek.

The crew: Captain Kleinschmidt, his wife, "Eskimos," and a motion-picture cameraman. Near the North Pole, they encountered Jimmy Aide, a dwarf. Jimmy declined a ride in the sleigh. He mounted Trouncer, the lead reindeer in the expedition's reindeer team. Jimmy piloted them across plains, to the crest of a slight rise. Whoa! The captain wrote:

> For the first time in the history of man, human beings were gazing upon the kingdom of Santa Claus. There before us on the rise in the snowy plain, bathed in moonlight, stood a glittering castle, its hundreds of towers as high as the mountains to the right and left. As the Northern Lights shone upon millions of windows, myriads [sic] of beautiful colors were reflected like sparkling gems. It was an overpowering sight. Never before in all my travels over the world have I witnessed such a sight.

It was, by all accounts, a sight. The cameraman captured the scene and the following week the *Free Press* announced that "Movies of Santa Expedition Will Start On Friday."

"Pictures of the Kleinschmidt expedition are said to be remarkable in every way," the paper wrote. "There are a number of thrilling scenes in the Arctic, and the climax shows the reception by Santa Claus and a trip through his castle and workshops."

Kids queued at the Metropolitan Theatre. Saturday's matinee sold out. The audience endured Mickey Mouse cartoons, Popeye cartoons, and a film starring the Dionne Quintuplets. Finally, the feature. A silent. Shots of walruses bawling — "Goblins of the North," according to the intertitle. Shots of a polar bear bathing — "Monarch of the North." Then, "Santa's snowy castle."

Captain Kleinschmidt was no captain. He and his wife ran a motion-picture production company in California. The articles about his expedition? Promotional copy newspapers printed to plug showings of the Kleinschmidts' film. A phony newsreel, *Santa Claus*.

The Kleinschmidts made *Santa Claus* in 1925 and showed it for years afterward. It was shot on sound stages in California, and on snowy plains in Alaska, where they hired Inuit to help build Santa's palace. Out of snow bricks. No glinting windows, no turrets. No roof.

Winnipeggers, I presume, weren't impressed.

Canada had seen snow castles, including the first snow castle constructed in North America. In 1904, one Constable Carey erected it in the yard of Rideau Hall. Two weeks, it took him, compressing tons of snow into blocks, piling snow block on snow block. Water was sprayed between. It froze into mortar. The castle's façade stood twenty-five feet high; the tower, thirty.

Canada had seen ice castles, including the first ice castle constructed in North America. Architects erected it in Montreal in 1883. A. C. Hutchison and his brother J. H. directed a crew of fifty men. Ice blocks cut from the St. Lawrence each weighed a quarter of a ton. Walls stood twenty feet high. The towers were fifty feet high. The main parapet topped out at ninety feet. The castle glowed "in a gorgeous aquamarine . . . the colors of auroral brilliance changed with each step the gazer took."

"Santa Claus will be in the Castle of Christmas Twinkles from 4 to 6 and 7 to 9 at night," announced an ad for Goodwin's of Montreal in 1919. Twinkles were polar fairies — Santa's Arctic helpers. Their enemies were the evil Twankles.

In 1933, the Hudson's Bay store in Winnipeg constructed an ice palace. Santa Claus's throne was upholstered in Hudson's Bay blankets. Morgan's of Montreal built an ice palace the following year. In 1940, Simpson's in Montreal advertised "jolly and nice, there's Santa Clause [sic] in his Palace of ice."

None of these palaces were really ice. "Ice" was made from siding or lath or plywood, painted silver. Fake snow was banked about. White felt was cut into icicles and sprinkled with mica. A photo in a 1946 issue of Simpson's *Staff News* shows two painters touching up a Toyland castle comprising two papier-mâché towers attached to a flat background.

Eric Field never saw a snow castle. Not as a kid. Field's from South Africa: Cape Town. "Christmas there was glitzy," he says. "Lots of colours. Lots of glitter. The sunshine hits it and just pops."

He became a commercial artist. Came to Canada in his twenties. He remembers the first Santa settings he saw. "Everybody was doing very traditional colours. It was boring." A couple years back, a client asked Field to design something different. It was then he conceived of his Arctic castle. A glittering crystal, "light and airy."

"I did the model first," he says, "then drew from that. My idea is the drawbridge — this whole thing is a drawbridge, everything happens on the drawbridge." The drawbridge consists of what looks like sheet ice. "I did the whole thing with a forced perspective, so it's very welcoming. These are like arms wide open."

At the end of the drawbridge sits a throne. Santa sits under an arch of ice. Turrets and towers spike from it. Behind the arch, a tree. "People think sometimes that design is pie in the sky," Field says. "Economics has a lot to do with the finished product. The budget dictates to me what I can do — transportation and putting it together. Because once we put it up, it's theirs after that. They have to put it up themselves."

I ask Eric Field what his house looks like at Christmastime.

"Everyone thinks I get these beautiful trees," he sighs. "They don't know how tired I am of Christmas." He's showing me the storeroom at Display Arts. Trees hang from nooses, already decorated. At Christmas, they'll be installed in bank towers and hospitals.

"I have these orange lights I put out on Halloween," he says. "I keep them until Christmas. I just plug them in and throw them on the floor and tippy-toe through them. That's it. That's Christmas."

"You could cut your foot," I say.

He laughs. "It's different if I go to my parents' place and they ask me to decorate. It's nice for them to do it. They only do it once a year."

9

SANTA PHOTOS

SNOW ON A tree. Snow on a rock. A young man stands in a field, snow-shoes slung over his shoulder.

"Young Canada" is the title of the photograph. William Notman shot it in 1867. In his studio. The snow on the studio floor is fur. Snow-white fox fur — the world's warmest fake snow. Warmest, and costliest.

"Specialties," Notman called them. Shots of subjects in staged sets. Notman erected a cottage in his Montreal studio to simulate summer shots. How did he simulate mosquitoes, I wonder? In his "Equestrian Court," subjects posed in sleighs and carriages. Subjects brought their horses, posed on horseback.

Winter costumes consisted of tuques and sashes. Subjects feigned snow-shoeing, skiing, skating, tobogganing. Sunlight was real, streaming through skylights.

Notman advertised his specialties in November newspapers. Specialties made especially nice Christmas gifts.

"The Christmas trade of the photographers and florists begins earlier than that of any other of the numerous and ever growing fraternity of those who cater to the world's wants," said the *Manitoba Free Press* in 1903. "The work of the photographer . . . begins early in October."

Photographs took time to print, tint, and mount. Photographers could only schedule one sitting at a time, could only photograph during daylight hours. Unless they had electricity. Wm. Notman & Son's 1900 ads promoted "Christmas Photographs for Business Men." Notman's son, William McFarlane, had taken over the studio. "If you cannot come while the daylight is good, we can photograph you by electric light."

Specialties had faded from style. Businessmen wanted businesslike portraits. Grey backdrops. Grey suits.

In 1902, Miss Wheeler hired Wm. Notman & Son to shoot her table settings. Its centrepiece: a feather tree. It was Christmas. Miss Wheeler set her table for six. Notman's photographed it during daylight. Even with electricity, residential rooms were too dim to shoot after dark. Dinner itself could not be recorded.

Notman's had dozens of employees and studios in twenty Canadian cities. Miss Wheeler lived in Montreal, as did Mr. Ballantyne. He retained Notman's in 1910 to shoot his great room. Decked out for a party — garlands, greens. A gala. Guestless. It was photographed at midday.

The photographer might have used magnesium flares. William Notman helped develop them. Flares combusted in coronas of light — instant exposures. Notman's of Montreal also captured Mr. Ballantyne's Christmas banquet of 1909. Mr. Ballantyne staged it in a ballroom. The studio set up several magnesium flares, covered in muslin shrouds, to diffuse light, contain smoke. Flares spewed clouds of it. In smaller spaces — dining rooms, for example — smoke spoiled supper, started fires. Don't burn magnesium near Christmas trees.

In the nineteenth century, photographers made pictures on plates of metal. "Tintypes," they were called, though the plates were copper. A chemical emulsion created the image, on the spot. Itinerant photographers barnstormed towns before Christmas, setting up studios in storefronts, shooting Christmas portraits for the less than wealthy. Working Canadians dressed in Sunday suits.

Many itinerant photographers worked carnival midways, snapping shots of couples. Tintype images which were then inserted into lockets and brooches. In the 1920s, tintypes were supplanted by paper pictures: postcard stock treated with chemicals. Photographers tramped door to door on Christmas morning, charging cash to take impromptu paper portraits. It was cold work. Film froze. Fingers, too.

Alberta journalist Harry M. Sanders has traced the history of Ed Brown, an itinerant photographer in Calgary. After the Second World War, Brown stood in the streets, snapping shots with roll film and a Kodak camera. "In the early days I used to snap wild, capturing nearly everybody that passed me," Brown said. He took up to a quarter million photos a year. Of families, of couples, of servicemen and servicewomen. Christmas was crazy. Brown stationed himself outside department stores, recording the rush. After snapping, he'd hand a subject a stub of paper — a negative number. The subject could then take the stub to a drugstore days later, and buy a print of the photo for fifty cents, or four for a dollar.

Brown's wife did the developing. Days in a darkroom.

In 1937, *Chatelaine* magazine offered "professional suggestions" for making a Christmas photo sitting successful: "While no photograph of you may ever look like Dolores Del Rio or Robert Taylor, you can get the best possible picture of YOU."

Some of the suggestions were obvious: "Allow plenty of time in which to arrive at the studio, and to recover from fatigue or weather conditions . . . Don't powder the nose too generously — it will be distorted . . . Don't remove eyeglasses . . . [a] lens is merciless in detecting eye defects."

Practise. That was *Chatelaine*'s main point. The magazine recommended that a subject practise posing in front of two mirrors, to find out "which half of your face is the better looking." To find out "whether your face is a little too thin or too long," or "whether or not your hands and arms are the size and shape to photograph effectively."

After studying yourself, after analyzing your ugliness, you must "try to overcome that strained look of expectancy or state of self-consciousness that spoils so many photographs."

"It's apt to be a terrifying experience, for wee people, sitting up in front of that great big, black camera," read a news story in the Montreal *Gazette* in 1939. It wasn't so much a news story as an ad dressed up as an article. An ad for Eaton's Christmas portraits: "Nakash, at Eaton's, says psychology secret of success." George Nakash was the chief por-trait photographer at Eaton's in Montreal. His technique for shooting tots? "Out come the toys — or the smiles and the jokes — or a little talk about the young one's likes, friends, or playthings."

Aziz George Nakashian, a Christian Armenian born in Mesopotamia, trained as a photographer at a department store studio in Beirut. World War I found him sheltered with family in Quebec. In 1918, he opened his own studio in Sherbrooke. "The Nakash Studio — Artistic Portraits."

The *Amateur Photographer and Cinematographer* of England awarded him a bronze medal in 1932, and Nakash decided to give the big city a go. He ran a studio in downtown Montreal for a few years, then took over the one on the ninth floor of Eaton's.

For years, Nakash acted as Eaton's resident photographer. He doc-umented graduations, weddings, anniversaries. And Christmases — in the Christmas shopping season, Nakash shot up to forty sittings a day. Montrealers in their Sunday best, sitters he posed carefully. He focused on hands. "You have beautiful hands!" he'd say. "You must show them!"

In 1919, Nakash sailed to the Middle East, returning with his young-est sister onboard. She'd survived the Turkish massacres of Armenians.

A few years later he helped bring his nephew to Canada — his older sister's son, Yousuf Karsh. Karsh was a teenager at the time. Nakash employed Karsh in his studio, gave Karsh a Brownie camera. Nakash then sent him to practise photography in Boston. Yousuf Karsh became, simply, Karsh, Canada's foremost photographer.

Karsh:

Nakash était un autodidacte, né dans un pays ou la notion d'image était reliée essentiellement a la poésie. Nakash choisit le langage l'homme, celui quie atteint l'universel, et il en fit un réussite.

Mon oncle Nakash fut mon premier maitre en photographie. Il était toujours disposé a partager ses connaissances.

[Nakash was self-taught, born in a country where the notion of imagery was largely related to poetry. Nakash chose the language of man, that which attains the universal, and with this he was very successful.

My uncle Nakash was my first photography teacher. He was always ready to share his knowledge.]

"Have your child in a Picture with Santa!" promised an ad for the Hudson's Bay Company's Winnipeg store in 1948. "The pictures make charming and unusual gifts for relatives and close friends."

Accompanying the ad was a photo of a bonneted girl sitting with Santa, smiling.

For decades, kids had visited Santa Claus, sat on his lap. Around World War II, parents started taking pictures. By then, cameras were portable, inexpensive. Flashbulbs were powerful enough to light Santalands. Department stores didn't like it. They barred amateur photography and installed professionals. At Eaton's, the Santa photographer shot every child who visited Santa. An elf distributed tickets to parents. "The T. Eaton Co. Limited has photographed your child with Santa Claus. To obtain copies, please fill in attached stub." Eaton's offered pick-up or delivery. A half dozen 3-by-4 portraits for fifty cents.

Eaton's portraits took a week to develop; that is, until Polaroid cameras came along in the 1960s. Eaton's slipped Polaroid pictures into Christmas cards cut to resemble picture frames. The upside: they developed in seconds. The downside: they've faded with time.

Santa's photographer — a new position in department stores. Many stores transferred an assistant from the in-store photo studio. In Calgary, the Hudson's Bay store hired Ed Brown, the sidewalk shutterbug.

Santalands began to incorporate photography stations. Photographers stood in booths, hidden behind wreaths and garlands. Children never saw them. "Children," said the *Bay Builder*, a magazine edited by employees at Vancouver's Hudson's Bay store, "were unaware that a hidden camera was taking a natural-looking portrait of them at the same time."

Wm. Prager Ltd. of Toronto built Santa chalets and Santa castles for malls across Ontario. Floor plans from the 1980s included Santa counters where parents purchased photographs. At the centres of the chalets stood sentry booths from which photographers shot their pictures.

Along with Santalands, Wm. Prager Ltd. sold Santa thrones, "ideal for photography." High-backed wooden chairs in white or woodgrain finish, with the seat and backrest padded in dark fabric. The dark fabric doubled as a backdrop for photos. Seats were wide enough to accommodate Santa and a couple of kids. A throne wasn't cheap — $1,000 was standard.

"Two years ago," photographer Bruce Lee says, "this man came in, looked like he had lots of money. A man of about fifty. He had his mother with him. His mother was ninety-three years old. It was her birthday. He'd said, 'Mom, what do you want on your birthday?' 'I want my picture taken with Santa Claus,' she said. He put her in the van, this little tiny woman, and took her to the mall. She was very bright with a big smile on her face. That's what she wanted. He said to me, 'I could've given her the world.'"

Bruce Lee shoots Santa photographs at the Avalon Mall in St. John's, Newfoundland. "One young couple came in. He'd arranged it so that he would ask his fiancée to marry him on Santa's lap. I had the camera, I took a number of shots as he took out the ring and proposed to her. I got seven shots off. I gave him a deal on the pictures.

"We get the young men and young women that have moved away, and they want to send their grandmother a picture. We get everybody from strippers to . . . well . . . we had the whole crew of the H.M.S. *Halifax*. Everybody loves Santa. Santa's like Elvis."

Bruce Lee's a Newfoundlander, born and bred. "My mom's got pictures," he says, "big black-and-white pictures of my two oldest brothers with Santa Claus. There were eight brothers. I'm fifth from the bottom, fourth from the top. By the time I came along, the trips to see Santa were getting a bit scarce."

The eldest Lee boys posed with Santa at the Woolworth's on Water Street in St. John's. "It was easy to tell he had a cheapie beard on him," Lee says of that Santa. "That's why, when I got into this business, I said, 'Well, there's two main things I'm going to concentrate on with Santa. First off, I'm going to pick the right person for the job, someone who loves children, and then, I'm going to dress him properly.'"

Photography's not Lee's bread and butter. "I'm a private investigator, so I had camera equipment already.

"This Santa idea came to me in the middle of the summer," he says. "I made an appointment and spoke to the manager of the Avalon Mall. And I said, 'I'll take that responsibility from you. I'll hire the Santas.' That's how I got started about five years ago. Usually what the malls do is hire some young fellow to be Santa. A mall here had a woman doing it one year. She didn't look the part. The kids were skinny and you'd see the plastic specs on them, cheap suits. It just looked tacky. What I did is took the classic Macy's Santa and had a tailor make the suit with all of the proper fur. I ordered the beards from a company in Toronto called Malabar. The boots alone, each pair is $500."

Word of mouth. That's how Lee found his Santas. "It took me a while to track them down. Trial and error. I just talked to them. I usually know. I got two excellent Santas this year. This one guy's a radio announcer. He had the voice. He knew different languages, and the different cultures of the kids. He could speak to the French kids. We get shoppers from St. Pierre, from Norway. We get all kinds of shoppers coming in."

Avalon Mall is Newfoundland's biggest, busiest mall. It already owned a deluxe Santa setting. "It's like a fantasy world," Lee says. "Great big oversized toys and fake snow. The kids' eyes are bouncing all over the place when they're in there. The whole idea is not only to take their picture, but to give them an experience.

"Santa will talk to them, sit them down, say, 'You're going to get a picture with the photographer.'" Lee carries a concealed horn, blasting it when he requires a child's attention. "The key to it is, within the first thirty seconds, to get a picture. In the first thirty seconds you'll get a spontaneous smile. After that, you'll see it going downhill real quick. Santa's got to be looking at exactly the same time. When I started, my timing was wrong."

A Santa photographer, says Lee, has to be born with patience, or learn it. "I take an average of maybe six to ten shots of each one. Other malls will do three shots and then say, 'That's it, you have to choose one of those.' I'll take as many as necessary — within reason. I never go beyond fifteen." He uses digital cameras and state-of-the-art dye-sublimation printers. "I can have the parent look at the screen, pick a picture, and within forty seconds they have it in their hands. That avoids a lot of problems."

Lee stays at the mall until late on Christmas Eve, "till the last smile leaves," he says. "I work forty-two days straight. I'm there every day, Derek. I've been there five years; they come there looking for me.

They come from out of town, from everywhere, from 200 miles away. They'll phone and make sure I'm there. Repeat customers are key. And I can remember these kids. I'm watching them grow up."

10

CATALOGUES

PLASTIC ICICLES. GLASS icicles. Tin. Tinkle. Flatiron's is a year-round Christmas store. Toronto's first. It opened in 1986.

Ted Genova owns it. He shows me around. There are blown-glass ornaments. Nativity sets under lock and key. Sets can sell for thousands. Madonna's playing on the stereo.

If it's Christmassy, it's here. Germany, Italy, America — Genova attends Christmas fairs and markets around the world, buying. He once commissioned a craftsman to carve a crèche based on the "Huron Indian Carol." An American bought it.

Genova takes me into his office. From a filing cabinet comes a folder. Inside the folder, a treasure. As a kid, Genova penned a letter to Saint Nick and posted it at a Santaland in an Eaton's store in Toronto.

Saint Nick wrote back.

Kids started writing Santa in the late nineteenth century. Winnipeg's post office processed a dozen or so such letters a year. *Santa Claus, North Pole* — that's how kids addressed them. Few bore stamps. Mail sorters sent them to the dead letter office. If letters had return addresses, they were returned. If they had none, they were destroyed.

A few families couldn't afford stamps. In 1925, Toronto's post office received 500 or so letters from kids in needy neighbourhoods. It turned them over to private philanthropists, people who'd agreed to fill the wish lists.

Five hundred — a fraction of the Santa letters the Toronto post office received in the 1920s. Toronto and every other town. Canada's Postmaster general had a problem. He was incinerating tens of thousands of Santa letters every year.

"The Postmaster-General," said a Canadian Press dispatch from 1929, "has now issued instructions that such letters are to be delivered to the big departmental stores where Santa Claus holds reception for some time before Christmas." Kids had also been sending Santa letters to department stores since the turn of the century, and stores had been answering them. In a 1903 ad, a Prairie department store reproduced a selection of letters they'd received. This, from a boy by the name of Robert McKissock:

> Dear Santy,
> I heard you had the measles, and hope that you will be better soon, so that you will be able to pay us a visit on Xmas day. I want you to bring me a pair of skates, a scrapbook, some candycanes, two soldier suits for myself, also a pair of skates, a little donkey, for my little brother, Charlie.

"Send Santa your correct name and address," said an ad for Goodwin's of Montreal in 1917. "He'll send you an autographed photograph of himself. He would like to know, though, what the colour of your eyes is."

Ted Genova of Flatiron's Christmas Market received his Santa letter from Eaton's. There's a colour illustration: Punkinhead sitting on Santa's lap. On Santa's desk, a letter: "I read your letter, very very carefully," it says, "and Punkinhead made sure your name is in my

Big Book of Good Boys and Girls. So just you wait until Christmas morning. . . ."

In 1946, Hudson's Bay Company Santa letters bore images of Santa at the North Pole. The Northern Lights bouncing off glacial mountains. The store sent them to the North Pole to be postmarked "North Pole, Alaska." The postal service returned them — "via reindeer," the store claimed.

"A special message from the North Pole." That's what Simpson's sent to kids who'd posted Santa letters to their Santaland in Toronto. Employees in the store's advertising department composed the message. Employees in the art department designed letters and envelopes.

Thousands of letters, sent to Ontario, Quebec, New York, Georgia. In 1945, the stationery was red and green, adorned with igloos. A pair of employees — Walter and Mildred Harrald, husband and wife — addressed the envelopes. By hand.

"We have letters from grown-ups who want Packard cars and mink coats," said Walter Harrald. "One businessman asked for a blonde!"

Adults didn't usually send letters to department stores.

Adults sent another sort of wish list.

In 1884, Eaton's issued a "Newspaper of Merchandise." Thirty-two pages, no pictures, printed on pink paper. The store distributed them to visitors at the Industrial Exhibition in Toronto, where it was showing off stock.

Visitors took them home to Quebec, Nova Scotia, Manitoba, then wrote to Eaton's, placing orders. Soon every store had a catalogue. Morgan's of Montreal. Woodward's of Vancouver. No season was as lucrative as Christmas. In 1899, an ad appeared in *The Halifax Herald*:

> The G. A. Holland & Son Co.'s of Montreal's New Christmas Catalogue with over 460 illustrations, Will be Sent Free to any address on receipt of 2c. postage stamp. As a book of interest it is worth all of a dollar, not to speak of the saving it will be to many to have our establishment brought to their very doors. It represents much of the genius of Japan, Germany, Austria, France, Great Britain, United States and Canada in the world of Dolls, Toys, Fancy Goods, Baskets, Games, Musical Instruments, Sporting Goods and hundreds of holiday presents.

Catalogues grew to hundreds of pages. Print runs swelled into the hundreds of thousands. By the 1920s, Canada had two major mail-order houses: Eaton's and Simpson's.

Simpson's had five stores. Through catalogues, they sold goods to millions of Canadians. Their catalogues catered to those living in suburbs and small cities. Fashion was their focus. They never sold plows or feed.

In 1920, the advertising manager for the Robert Simpson Company delivered a talk to the managers and assistant managers of the mail-order department in Toronto. "The catalogue," he said, "is the only sales factor to bring in the vast amount of business necessary to maintain this tremendous organization."

Simpson's printed catalogues in the basement of its Toronto store. "The most economical way, in time and cost, is to have as many forms of sixty-four pages as possible," the advertising manager said. A cylinder press could print 2,000 forms per hour. Two cylinder presses ran twenty-two hours per day for nine months to produce sufficient copies. Colour forms were printed on flatbed presses, then "tipped" — inserted by hand — into the black-and-white forms. "In a catalogue, such as the one just printed, close to 25 million pieces of color work have to be inserted." The work was done by women — "girls," the advertising manager called them — "who do nothing but this and so become proficient and rapid."

Gathering machines gathered forms. Stitching machines stitched. After a cutting machine trimmed edges, a conveyor belt carried catalogues to the mail room. A representative of the post office toiled year round in Simpson's cellar. He or she addressed catalogue wrappers, then planned routes. Fifty carloads of catalogues left Toronto in the fall "for delivery at practically every Post Office from the Atlantic to the Pacific."

Frederick Brigden Sr. was born in Britain. He studied under artist and philosopher John Ruskin. In 1871, he emigrated to Toronto and cofounded the Toronto Engraving Company Ltd., which came to be known as Brigden's Ltd.

After 1901, Eaton's produced its catalogue in its own printing department. But for illustrations, it went to Brigden's. Brigden's, in turn, developed its own specialized staff of mail-order artists. Up to eighty artists worked on the Christmas catalogues.

To cater to their western clientele, Eaton's decided to put out a version of their catalogue — featuring farm equipment — specifically styled for the western Canadian. In 1914, Brigden's son, Frederick H., established Brigden's of Winnipeg.

The top three floors of the Farmer's Advocate Building were occupied by Brigden's. More than 100 artists worked here. In winter, artists diluted paint with glycerine to keep it from freezing. For magnifying glasses, they used jars of water. In winter, the water iced over. The Christmas catalogue was produced in summer. Stifling summer.

A Christmas catalogue took three months to make. An artist sketched a product; another artist coloured the sketch. Another added details. Engravers carved it into woodblocks. Catalogue season, illustrator Charles Comfort once said, was "a prolonged, violent and eccentric convulsion, a noisy, frenetic, helter-skelter struggle against time and deadlines."

Comfort started work at Brigden's in Winnipeg during the First World War. He was fifteen. Some illustrators drew only shoes, others only bracelets. Comfort drew farm machines. A 1927 plow was captioned: "Do your Shares Wear out quickly? Then, if so, you are riding the wrong gang!" During the Second World War, Comfort went overseas as a war artist with the Canadian Active Service Force. In Italy, he witnessed the Battle of Ortona. In Canada, he painted it. *Canadian Armour Passing through Ortona* hung at the National Gallery in Ottawa, an institution Comfort directed from 1960 to 1965.

Comfort was by no means the only celebrated artist to work at Brigden's. Brigden's hired Hal Foster in 1913. Foster stayed for eight years, then went to America to draw Tarzan comic books. He invented his own comic strip, *Prince Valiant*, which ran in thousands of newspapers across the continent. Charlie Thorson worked at Brigden's on and off for twenty years, from the 1920s to the 1940s. He also worked for Hollywood. For Disney, he sketched Snow White and the Seven

Dwarfs. For Warner Brothers, he sketched the original Bugs Bunny. He also designed Punkinhead for Eaton's. Pauline Boutal and Christiane Le Goff were sisters who stayed at Brigden's for decades. Boutal designed sets and costumes for Le Cercle Molière theatre troupe of St. Boniface. Le Goff became known as "the best fashion artist in Canada."

My favourite catalogues came from Dupuis Frères, the Montreal department store. "*Catalogue entièrement français publié par une maison possédée et administrée par des Canadien-Français,*" the cover of their 1931 publication announced proudly. It boasts a statue of Dollard des Ormeaux, a seventeenth-century garrison commander of the fort at Ville-Marie.

The Dupuis Frères catalogues sold articles not found in Eaton's books. Religious accoutrements, for example — "*Soutanes, surplis, crucifix, etc.*" Crucifixes glowed in the dark, as did statues of saints Antoine, Anne, and Thérèse-de-l'Enfant-Jésus. The 1951–52 catalogue offered a range of children's items inspired by Maurice "Rocket" Richard. Best of all was a zipper-front, belted, three-quarter coat in satin gabardine. The coat's front panels featured an illustration of Richard shooting a puck into a net as a helpless goalie looks on. A goalie in a Leafs jersey. The artists? Unknown.

Woodward's founded a mail-order catalogue department on the fifth floor of their Vancouver store. Woodward's catalogue carried "the message of our low prices, quality merchandise and service to rural B.C., Yukon, Alberta, Saskatchewan and points all over the world." In 1950, the Woodward's employee magazine featured a photo layout of the catalogue department. It seems that no more than ten people toiled there. Mr. Wood managed the office. He's pictured in a meeting with Mr. Tawnsley of Johnson's Wax.

Miss Edith Leach laid out pages. Miss Claire Golder retouched them. Miss Ida Boshier, Mr. Markell, and Mr. Evans worked on copy. Mr. Weekes shot merchandise in the photo studio, "surrounded by equipment rivalling a Hollywood Movie Set."

Photography had now overtaken illustration. Eaton's contracted production of its eastern catalogues to Pringle & Booth, who specialized in catalogue photography. Brigden's let illustrators go and hired photographers. The Winnipeg Blue Bombers modelled menswear for Eaton's western catalogue. College girls modelled unmentionables.

"There's very little illustration," says Roy Harrold of Sears Canada. Harrold works on the Sears Christmas Wish Book. "It used to be a layout artist who actually drew most of the layouts — drew them and coloured them. Now the illustration is used on details. Instead of having a cross-section where you actually cut the product, illustration will show the details. But other than that, not a lot of illustration, no. The layouts are sketched by artists, but not anywhere to the detail they were."

In the 1950s, Sears, Roebuck and Co. was the biggest mail-order company in the United States. It wanted to be the biggest in Canada, to beat Eaton's. In 1953, it formed an affiliation with Simpson's. Simpson's kept its stores, which were all located in large cities. Sears would open stores in suburbs and smaller cities. The two firms — operating as Simpsons-Sears — would share a catalogue. Its first Wish Book came out in 1953. Seven hundred pages, a tenth of them filled with toys.

"I can remember personally shopping from the Sears catalogue," Harrold says. "I grew up in B.C., close to Burnaby, where our big expedition every year was to go in and pick up our parcels at the catalogue warehouse.

"I started in Edmonton in our retail store." That was thirty-six years ago. "Then I moved to headquarters, into the buying department." The headquarters is in Toronto, on Jarvis Street. "I was assistant buyer, buyer, marketing manager." He's now National Manager, Online Media Planning.

"When I got here we used 35-mm photos. There were a lot of hard copies of pages and layouts. The film would come to us looking like negatives; they were coloured, coloured stills. Probably fifteen years ago there was a big transition to computers. And in the last eight or nine years, we converted to Mac computers.

"We've got around 200 people who were involved in producing the 2004 Wish Book. All of them are full-time. There's no photographic studio here. Our advertising company has the photography studio . . . actually a few studios, photographers on staff, copywriters, editors, layout artists. Then there are a lot of people involved with being responsible for actually making sure the pages flow through. They're involved with scheduling, with set-up, with helping the photographers, moving the pages through production."

Production begins in March. Pages go out to the printer in June. Sears prints its catalogues in Toronto — millions of copies at a thousand or so pages per. "Because the book is so big," Harrold says, "it's printed over a long period of time. And then all the forms are collected and bound at the end. And it takes almost ten weeks to print." Planning for a Christmas catalogue starts in November of the previous year. I talked to Harrold before Christmas 2004. He was already thinking about Christmas 2005. "You can get Christmased out," Harrold admits. "It's almost like Christmas is continual."

In the 1970s, fewer and fewer children saw Santa at department stores. More and more saw him at shopping malls. Malls didn't reply to kids' mail. By the 1980s, Santa letters were piling up at post offices. In Montreal, a few postal workers decided to answer them. The public appreciated it. Canada Post appreciated the appreciation, and announced an official Santa letter program in 1982 — to be run by "elves," meaning employees and retired employees.

Don Capalbo worked at Canada Post for thirty-five years, retiring in 1999. But he did not retire from the Santa program, which he'd been doing for seventeen years. Capalbo was named co-ordinator for all Ontario elves. "[In Ontario] we have 400 volunteers answering letters this year," he told *Saturday Night* magazine. "This morning, I woke up at four and answered forty-five letters."

"We don't promise anything," Capalbo explained. Girls wanted ponies. Boys, bikes. Capalbo would write back with encouraging words and compliments. "We won't write, 'P.S. Mary, you'll get your pony.'" Letters came from kids in hospitals. Capalbo forwarded them to aid agencies. When letters came from kids living in poverty, Capalbo forwarded the letters to charitable agencies like *The Toronto Star*'s Santa Claus Fund.

Capalbo is one of 13,000 elves answering letters. By the Santa program's twentieth anniversary, over 11 million replies had been posted, in twenty-six different languages. And Braille.

"Every letter has to be read," Capalbo said. "Every one."

11

HOLLY AND MISTLETOE

As a kid, I visited Vancouver. A family trip. Ask any member of my family, "What do you remember about British Columbia?" We'll all say the same thing: the holly tree in Stanley Park.

In late summer. Red and green. Christmassy. My folks had never seen a holly tree. I'd never seen real holly.

At our house, holly was hazardous. It was plastic. My mother twined vines of it around lamps, table legs. The vines had plastic tabs where they'd been cut. Leaves had spiny ridges, sharp enough to prick skin. Mom used the holly for decades. She threw it out only a couple years ago. It's landfill, now. Not rotting.

Fake holly lasts forever. And it's existed forever. "Imitations can be made which answer all the purposes of the real ones," a newspaper columnist wrote in 1882. The author suggested wrapping peas in red cotton. The best cotton: turkey-red. Other options included putty rolled into balls and coloured with a mix of sealing wax and spirits of wine. "Easiest of all, artificial berries are sold in bunches very cheaply at most toy shops."

Some Canadians couldn't get to toy shops. Like Catharine Parr Traill. She lived in rural Ontario. In 1838, she was pining for "the bright varnished holly and its gay joy-inspiring red berries" she'd known in England. She sent her maid down to the shore of Rice Lake to fetch cranberries. Berries — be they cranberries or ivy berries — will keep when soaked in strong salt water. Parr Traill affixed them to fir boughs. "With the red transparent berries of the cranberry [we] were obliged therefore to content ourselves. . . ."

Some Canadians hung real holly. Some holly came from Europe, boxed and shipped on steamships. Havre to Liverpool. Liverpool to New York. Then it was loaded onto northbound trains.

Some holly came from England. In the early 1880s, a Halifax wholesaler advertised a shipment of "English Holly in first-class condition." A Montreal vendor advertised "[a] shipment of 20 cases of holly . . . received from England almost as fresh as when cut from the tree."

An unlikely claim. English and European holly reached Canada in wretched condition. Berries were rolling around. Leaves were shrivelled, or blackened.

Holly heaped on tables. Holly hanging from rafters. Wreaths and garlands and sprays. A Christmas Bazaar. That's what Eaton's Toronto store called their seasonal sections in the early 1900s. The holly was American, harvested in holly-growing states — Virginia, North Carolina, the topmost part of Texas.

American holly differs from European and English holly. It's smaller, not as green. Maryland holly was known as "Triple X." Canadians considered it inferior to southern holly. Maryland holly grew on hills, southern holly in shade. All American holly reached Canada with its berries intact. And it was cheap.

The peninsula between Delaware and Chesapeake produced tons of holly every year. Kids cut it weeks before Christmas. They climbed holly trees, which topped out at thirty feet. The children chopped branches that had berries. The branches fell. Sometimes the kids did, too. Other kids gathered the branches off the ground, broke them into smaller branchlets, then bagged them.

At home, kids bunched the berries — two or three sprigs each, tied with wire. The wire cut their fingers. So did the holly. Holly leaves are leathery, with thorny spikes. Older girls wound wreaths of sweet pepper bush, azalea, grapevine — pliable plants. Then they attached the holly. The more berries, the higher the cost of the wreath.

Villagers displayed their wreaths in yards and on porches. Dealers drove by, buying at six and a half cents per wreath. Some villagers traded wreaths at the local store. For cash, or food. Holly dealers loaded wreaths in boxes and crates and shipped them north. Some shipped wreaths woven from black alder leaves. A scam — the berries broke off. Other dealers bought more holly than they could sell, incinerating the surplus, thus denying it to competitors. Holly burns hot. It contains oil. Fling it on a fire and it vanishes in burly black smoke.

Mistletoe was much the same. Early Canadians imported mistletoe from France — the forests of Fontainbleau — in the early nineteenth century. It was expensive. It was fragile. European mistletoe has green berries. By the time it got here, the berries were black. Suitable for Halloween.

As with holly, an American mistletoe market opened up. Mistletoe grows in southern states on elm trees. Also on pecan, hickory, oak, mulberry, apple, pear, cherry, and water ash. From Missouri to Oklahoma, kids scaled trees to cut down mistletoe. It sold with bits of bark attached.

Kids could get hurt. Not just falling from trees, or cutting themselves — mistletoe is toxic if swallowed; the berries can be lethal.

In 1916, *Scientific American* declared mistletoe an insidious pest. Exterminate it, they suggested.

Mistletoe berries ripen in fall. Birds eat the berries, excrete the seeds. The seeds stick to new trees. Sprout. The plant's feelers burrow into bark, where they siphon water and minerals and food the tree's created. They give nothing back. Mistletoe is a parasite, or at least a semi-parasite. It makes some of its own food. It contains chlorophyll, which transforms sunlight into sugar.

Mistletoe stunts tree growth. Enough mistletoe will kill a tree. Goldthwaite, Texas, is the mistletoe capital of North America. Farmers hack off mistletoe to sell at Christmas. Farmers hack it off to keep the trees alive.

Holly trees live forever. Almost. Hundreds of years, anyway. A tree won't bear any crop until it's a decade old. A century-old tree will bear tons of holly in its lifetime. Pare a tree too bare — it dies. It happened in the States. The holly industry overcut its wild holly trees, so the industry went commercial. Holly was produced by professionals in nurseries in Oregon and Washington.

And in British Columbia. Holly trees need warm weather and high humidity; coastal climates provide them. British Columbia's the only place in Canada where conditions are correct. In 1851, a surveyor working for the Hudson's Bay Company planted English holly on Vancouver Island — the first English holly trees in Canada.

G. H. Hadwen hailed from England. He studied agriculture in Guelph, Ontario, then in 1890 settled on a farm, Amblecote Estate, near Duncan, British Columbia, planting holly trees he'd brought from his homeland. He had a few male trees, many female. Female trees bear berries.

At Christmas 1895, Hadwen sold his first holly harvest, shipped by train to stores as far east as Winnipeg. Other farmers founded their own orchards in the 1920s with cuttings from Hadwen's farm. Their wares went to Ontario and Quebec, the country's main holly markets. Farmers tried different breeds. Silver and gold holly were hot for a spell. Funeral homes buy it now.

G. H. Hadwen died in 1952. His daughter inherited Amblecote Estate. She passed it on to her son, whose name is Gaylard.

"I'm a lawyer," says Gaylard Hadwen. "I gave up lawyering to run the holly farm."

"Do you miss it?"

"I don't miss it at all," he says. He's sitting with me in his office. The Okanagan Valley lies beyond us. Mount Malahat. "Divorces and car accidents. I had enough of that.

"My grandfather planted these trees," he says, ambling around Amblecote. Hadwen guesses he's got 1,200 trees. "These are the flowers." It's May. He shows me white petals. Later, green berries will grow, then redden.

Hadwen and his wife Helma also raise chickens. Chicken dung fertilizes holly. "It's just like any farming thing. Insect problems." Moths. Maggots. "The one that causes problems is phytophera." A fungus. "It affects holly when it's wet. It can defoliate. Turn berries black."

Come October, Gaylard hires a crew to harvest the holly. "The most we've ever shipped is 46,000 pounds. Varies tremendously according to how good of a year it is." Ten pickers clip the holly. Ten packers pack it. Ten-pound boxes ship to wholesale florists. Half-pound bags sell in grocery stores in Toronto.

Is holly poisonous?

"No," he says. "I've heard that, but it's not poisonous. Not like mistletoe. When I was a little kid, my mother used to take me up in the holly. She was the boss of the pickers. She put me in a crib and I used to eat the berries all the time. "Didn't hurt me."

He laughs. "Maybe it did!"

12

TREES

1.

A TREE IN a field. My sister and I agreed: it was good.

Dad strapped it to the station wagon. Mom paid. I drank hot chocolate. Ate snow off my mittens. Tasted like wool.

Did Dad chop the tree down? What kind of tree? Pine? Spruce? I don't remember. It was, my parents tell me, my only trip to a Christmas tree farm. I was five.

I decide to go back. I drive north to visit the farm I visited as a kid. Dad gives me directions, the air conditioner blowing like it's November.

NO TRESPASSING.

I trespass. I'm alone in a field. Me and the mosquitoes. They hang like netting around my head. It smells outdoorsy. There's a snake fence, there's a shed. Nothing in it. Weeds growing like weeds.

And trees — bushy, goosenecked. A gooseneck's a section of trunk that doesn't grow any whorls. A whorl's a bunch of branches.

These trees, I think, are uncultured.

I drive down the road to a house. Vi Hall meets me. Vi's short for Violet. She and her late husband, Roy, ran the farm. I ask if she remembers me.

"Little kid?" I say. "Yay high? In snowpants? Real excited about Christmas?"

"Lots of people called and came by," she says. "We never advertised. We just put trees in the yard."

So Dad didn't cut down our tree?

"No, Roy would've done that."

Did you serve hot chocolate?

"No, none of that. There's a tree farm up on the highway where you can get hot chocolate. Here it's just trees."

What to give Her Highness who has everything? A tree. Prince Albert gave one to Queen Victoria at Christmas 1841. They'd been married for a year. In Germany, Christmas trees were a yuletide tradition. In England, they weren't. Albert hailed from Germany. He gave Victoria a Norway spruce.

"The new German way of celebrating Christmas." That's how a Toronto newspaper referred to Christmas trees in the late 1850s. Wealthy Canadians mimicked their monarch. According to a Victorian journalist, Canadians "acquired their Christmas tree . . . by the simple expedient of telling their manservant to go out to the woods at the edge of the city and cut one."

Some Canadians didn't have manservants. Some didn't have trees. Albertans, for example, who'd settled the plains. No trees or towns for miles. *Christmas in the West* relates the tale of a family from Scandia, south of Brooks, who in 1918 "gathered a big bunch of Russian thistle, or tumbleweed, placed it in the corner of their two-room home, and decorated it with Christmas ornaments."

Some families didn't have whole trees. Near the timberline, north winds strip needles from the north sides of pines. South sides survive. Catherine McKinnon, a writer and singer born near James Bay, remembered cutting down two trees and tying them together to make one.

"When Roy went to get the cows and that, he'd prune a tree a bit with a jackknife," Vi says. "And that's how it started." I'm in Vi's kitchen. A farmhouse on a tree farm. A thousand acres in the Canadian Shield. Forests forever. Here and there, lakes.

"Roy lumbered," she says. "All his life he worked in the woods. We paid for the place by cutting cordwood. Three dollars and fifty cents a bush cord. Dry maple, body maple. Two seventy-five if it had limbs in it.

"Some of them from the Forestry in Bancroft, they'd come down and ask Roy to show them places. They said he knew every tree in the woods."

Until the 1870s, the Blackfoot hunted buffalo in Alberta, trading the furs. Then the buffalo died out. Whisky had appeared, and poverty. The Canadian government talked Blackfoot bands into signing Treaty 7, creating a reserve at Blackfoot Crossing in southern Alberta. The government gave them one square acre per family, five bucks per person per year, and a plow for each band.

An Anglican clergyman founded a mission on the reserve. In 1883, he noted that the Blackfoot had discovered a money-making venture: selling Christmas trees to white settlers. Lodgepole pines.

In the Vancouver City Archive, Major J. S. Matthews deposited a document describing the ways Canadians found Christmas trees: "There was no Christmas tree problem before the Great War; it was more a matter of 'Where shall we go to get one.'" Fields, forests. A favoured spot was Indian reserves.

"But one day, I recall the first occasion, when, at Kitsilano Beach we took a small axe and started off, with the children, to cut a Christmas tree in the Indian Reserve." He did not cut a tree because the trees had all been cut. That was in 1913.

According to Matthews, a Christmas tree industry cropped up in British Columbia after the Great War. "There were men who went out and gathered Christmas trees; just one or two, and, if memory serves correctly, the first I saw was a man who had a few stacked together" in a public square in Vancouver.

"The street-corner Christmas tree trade developed until, about 1935 or so, men contested for street corners." Trees were a hard sell in the Great Depression. When a tree seller stole another's spot, shouting matches erupted, or fist fights. Cops were called.

"During the last days of November, or early days of December, 1939, I was walking toward the City Hall, and saw a large group of men — probably thirty — waiting in the rain." Matthews approached one of the men, asking, "'What's all the excitement?' His reply astonished me; it was, 'Getting permits to sell Christmas trees.'"

"We sold wild ones at first," Vi says. "We cleared a lot of fields where there were trees already coming in. At one time, we sold two or three thousand trees."

Roy cut them all himself. "The bigger trees you had to tie. You get a twenty- or thirty-foot spruce, that would go to department stores or shopping malls. We sent several down to Union Station.

"I dug these out for you," Vi says, emptying an envelope. Ribbons. Blue ribbons. "These are from the Royal Winter Fair. Roy got these. This is the tree that won first prize." Best tree of 1969. "I don't know what happened to it after the fair. Someone took it home."

The Halls supplied trees to tree lots, grocery stores, and malls in southern cities. "The buyers would come in early and see what they wanted. When they got to know Roy, they'd just phone their orders in. We had one group that came that would tie them and take a look at them. My, oh my, the trees they picked." She shakes her head. Snorts. "We wouldn't have cut them!"

Potatoes. Apples. That's what Maritime farmers farmed until the 1920s, until they realized they had another crop — trees — growing wild on pastureland. Balsam firs were textbook Christmas trees. Blue-green, needles stiff enough to hold ornaments. A good tree could bring a dime. Farmers cut them down and trucked them to towns and cities.

New York City needed trees. Boston needed trees. Baltimore. The Hofert Company of California set up shop in Moncton. Hofert agents spread out across Nova Scotia, New Brunswick, and Quebec, buying firs which they shipped to cities across the northern United States.

Before trees left, some Maritimers tied begging messages to branches. A man in New Jersey "found a note from Phyllis McFarlane of New Brunswick attached to a tree in a shipment he had ordered from Canada. It was addressed to Santa, and asked for a doll, sled, set of dishes, candy and nuts." Begging notes looked bad on railways. It wasn't hard to catch the culprits. They wrote their addresses on the notes.

In 1937, the *Imogene*, a Hofert steamer, docked in Montreal. Its cargo was a quarter of a million firs bound for Minnesota. Maritime farmers reaped old growth until there was little old growth left to reap. Then came competition: trees grown in the States in nurseries. "Artificial" trees, they were called then.

Atlantic Canada was slow to start nurseries. Ontario was not. Ontario farmers cultured trees, from seed to sapling to sawing, employing scientific methods of planting, pruning, and reaping. Ontario farmers specialized in Scotch pine. Scotch pines grow in all sorts of soil — sandy, gravelly. They grow fast and smell piney. And they have no other uses — not in construction, not in papermaking.

Vi and Roy Hall sold spruce and balsam. "Myself, I liked spruce," Vi says, "but then I graduated to balsam because they hold the needles a lot better. A lot of Europeans grew up with the balsam, and that's what they liked when they came over after the war." We're standing outside her home.

"Then we did plant some Scotch pines. We never did like the Scotch pines as good as we did the other trees. If you go to decorate them, they're very dense. They're hard on the hands and that. The government would raise a lot of trees and you could buy them from the government quite reasonably."

I'm sweating. Scotch pines aren't shade trees. Vi's trees haven't been pruned in a decade, not since Roy died.

"Austrian pines grew different," she says. "They're stiff, and their needles seemed so much sharper. You weren't supposed to have to prune them. But they really went crazy if you didn't. They never really caught on. It's a good thing. I hated them."

In the 1950s, a few farmers founded the Ontario Christmas Tree Growers Association, the first of its kind in the country. It published a manual for prospective tree farmers:

> Are you thinking of starting a Xmas tree farm? If so, you should first consider this: The people you wish to join have been variously described as "that fellow who wears the yellow rain suit and doesn't know enough to come in out of the rain," "that guy stuck in the snow on the 6th Concession hill with a truckload of trees," or "that couple who flail away at trees with long knives on a hot July weekend when they could be at the beach."

That was page one. The next fifty drove home the point: tree farming is tricky.

A farmer leases land. Nothing too rocky, nor rolly. It's sandy, but not too sandy. A sure sign of poor soil: poverty grass. The farmer burns hardwood brush. He plows ferns under. He digs out rocks.

He plants a few acres with seedlings from a nursery. Thousands of them. He heels them in; that is, he plants them along the sloping side of a shallow V-shaped trench that he's dug himself. In a decade, he has his first cash crop. Maybe.

Dry spells hit in spring and fall. The farmer digs firebreaks, keeps fire departments on call. Tree farms can be fire traps. New shoots are known as "candles."

Harsh winters hurt the trees. Ice snaps branches. Snow burns needles brown. Scotch pines yellow in late summer, and no one wants yellow trees. So the farmer spray paints them with paint he buys from a tree-farm supplier. Green, or blue-green, a vegetable dye that allows trees to photosynthesize. The dye washes off after a year or so.

A truck backs up to the tree farm at night. Men with handsaws slip into the stand, sawing. They load up the truck with trees.

The farmer can't fight thieves. How does he prove that a certain tree is his? He could match stumps, if he had weeks to do it. Some farmers guard their trees with guns. More than one thief has died trying to steal a spruce.

Some farmers have experimented with sprays, spritzing them on trees they don't intend to harvest. If a perfumed tree should be stolen and set up indoors, the spray will warm up, activate. It's made from skunk oil and garlic.

Birds eat tree berries. Mice eat bark, as do rabbits. Girdling, it's called. The water's cut off and the tree dies from the top down. Deer feed on new shoots and needles. A deer can trample a seedling. Bears can trample saplings. The farmer sets a trap, snares skunks, and porcupines.

He tries scaring the animals with noise. "Jingle Bells" blasting day and night, by Alvin and the Chipmunks.

The farmer fights weeds growing between trees. He scalps the soil. He spies a tree that's covered with soot. But it's not soot, it's mould. The tree's infected with spittlebugs. Spittlebugs eat needles. As they eat, they secrete foam, white and light, like spring snow. Mould grows on their excrement.

The farmer panics. Plucks a bug from a branch. He drops it in a little box, the kind jewellery stores sell, and mails it to Ottawa. The Ministry of Environment. He gets a letter back: DON'T SEND LIVE BUGS.

The farmer sprays his trees with pesticide, which makes his trees more flammable. He vanquishes his spittlebugs.

Then come roundworms, spinning silky threads as they devour trees. Aphids that deposit sugary droppings on branches. The droppings attract ants, which eat bark, causing cankers in the trunk. The farmer sprays more pesticide. Upwind. If he sprays too much pesticide, the trees might turn white, or orange. If he inhales it, he could die. He keeps an antidote handy — two parts activated charcoal, one part magnesium oxide, one part tannic acid. That's supposed to save him.

The farmer hopes his pesticide works. If it doesn't, his trees could be quarantined. Which means he's just spent the last decade grooming firewood.

"The worst thing," says Vi, "is the pruning." Christmas trees aren't born, they're bred. A tree farmer has to cut his crops into cones. The classic Christmas tree shape — taper, tree farmers call it. The ideal is a tree that's 60 percent wider at the base than at the top.

"We had a lot of wild trees, so we'd have to cut the brush around the trees. We started with machetes, then we did shears. When a Scotch pine got to be nearly six foot high — when it was ready to go — we counted 200 snips to a tree. That's what it took to try and get it shaped just right."

Fir flies. Pines are sticky. Pitch sticks to skin, insects to pitch. Blackflies, deer flies, mosquitoes. A fast farmer can shear hundreds of trees in a day. A typical tree farm has thousands of trees. Roy and Vi hired helpers in the summer and at Christmastime. I tell her about a friend of a friend who stabbed himself in the knee on his first day of Christmas tree pruning.

"It can be hard," she says. "You have to remember to swing the machete away from you."

"Another reason to buy fake trees," I say.

"I never let one of those in the house," Vi says.

2.

Do Christmas trees trigger allergies? Yes, or so said Canadian doctors in the 1970s, when a large group of their patients "developed attacks of sneezing and wheezing several days after installing Christmas trees."

My mother took my sister and me to the doctor. He scratched me, rubbed the scratch with a powder made up of ground-up white pine, red pine, Australian pine, Scotch pine, Norway spruce, blue spruce, and juniper. A red bump rose. Rudolph's nose — on my back.

My sister reacted, too. Real Christmas trees? We'd always had them, but we never got another.

CHRISTMAS DAYS

In the 1880s, German authorities tried to save fir forests by banning Christmas trees. Germans decided to make their own. The branches they made from wire. For fir, they glued feathers to the branches. Swan, turkey, or goose feathers, dyed green. The feathers didn't look much like needles. The frames didn't look like trees. Not any trees I've seen.

Germans carried the trees to Canada, where they made new ones, with Canadian geese. Geese don't like to be plucked, so they're strangled and cooked for Christmas. Feathers were washed. Feathers are full of allergens. Geese have dander.

In the 1930s, the Addis Brush Company created an artificial Christmas tree from toilet brushes. The trunk: a broomstick painted green. Brushes were branches — wire handles slotted into the broomstick. Trees came in a couple of shades of green: Ponderosa pine, Appalachian fir.

And red. There were red trees, and white trees, which proved popular with window trimmers. Addis brushes were made of hair — horse hair, squirrel hair, badger hair. Hair is also allergenic. By the 1950s, most brush decorations were plastic. My grandmother decorated her house with red toilet brush wreaths the size of toilet seats.

In the 1960s, Eaton's in Toronto built a space-age Santaland. Santa sat on a throne, in what looked like NASA's control room. A fifteen-foot rocket stood nearby on a launching pad. Kids climbed into it, pretending to fly to the moon. Everything — the control station, the spaceship — was silver, including the Christmas trees.

In 1959, the Aluminum Novelty Company of Mantiwoc, Wisconsin, invented aluminum trees. Mantiwoc was then known as the "Aluminum Cookware Capital of the World." The trees were a sales sensation.

Noma Ltd. got into the aluminum tree game. Noma was an American firm with branch plants in other countries. In 1959, Noma's Toronto factory started manufacturing aluminum Christmas trees for the Canadian market.

Machines shredded sheets of aluminum, which were then wrapped around wires. Shreds were needles. Workers fluffed them by hand. Fluffers, they were called. They wore leather gloves. Wood ornaments, popcorn garlands, paper snowflakes — these old ornaments looked awful on aluminum trees. Noma sold colour wheels, which sat beneath the tree, projecting light. Red, gold, green. Red, gold, green.

"The aluminum ornaments have gradually taken a percent of the market and have appealed to a certain clientele," sniffed a report from a Canadian Christmas tree farmers' association in the 1960s. "Ornaments." That's what they called fake trees. "However, their everlasting qualities have been somewhat overplayed, and there is evidence that they will never take the place of the live tree."

Tree farmers hedged their bets. They appealed to fake tree buyers by making real trees look fake. As early as the 1930s, florists were experimenting with silver trees — that is, trees dipped in a solution of water and alum. "For the home done in the modern style," said an interior designer. An article in a 1940s science magazine profiled a company that sold live potted pines, ideal for apartment dwellers. The trees were dipped in silver or gold paint, which killed them.

A tree growers' manual suggested spraying trees where they grew on the farm. Browning trees could be turned green. Or orange. Or yellow. "Even such exotic hues as pink are found for those who want something unusual."

John H. Rice worked at Noma Canada for years. In the early 1960s, he left and founded his own firms: Carillon and Alderbrook Industries. He released a revolutionary tree that looked like no other fake tree before it: realistic.

Rice introduced polyvinyl chloride (PVC), a stainproof, fireproof synthetic. He wove threads of extruded PVC with threads of wire. The result? A Scotch pine that looked like a Scotch pine.

It soon became Canada's best-selling artificial tree. Noma canned their aluminum line, started making PVC pines. Noma made them with outswept branches, upswept branches, or inswept branches. There were different colours: dark green, light green, dark green with light green tips. Lighter tips look like new growth.

My grandmother put up a Noma Scotch pine at Christmastime. Real pines have hard needles, but so do fakes. Don't decorate one with bare arms. It's like taking an allergy test.

Barcana, a German firm, built a plant in Quebec in the 1970s. A decade later, it introduced fake soft-needle firs — eastern and green balsams. Soft-needles sold sensationally. Barcana also warrantied trees for a decade. The average artificial tree lasts for six years.

Noma introduced their own soft-needle models. They hired a team of twenty-five tree decorators who travelled across the country to decorate store trees. Noma also experimented with pine-scented sprays. "Most artificial odours end up smelling like Lysol," said Andrew Rafelman, Noma's marketing manager.

"It's like fashion," Malca Langer tells me. "One year we would have green, and people would want white trees. So the next year we would buy millions of white trees and they would sit here. We would buy purple trees. This year, for instance, pink is going to be the big thing."

Malca Langer is a Prager. Her father founded Wm. Prager Ltd., a Toronto display store, in 1938. Prager's sell props to display designers. "I've been here since I was fifteen years old," Langer tells me, "so I'm a real fixture. People like to come in and see someone that they recognize, that's been here a long time.

"There were very few of us in the display trade back then," Langer says. "There really was nobody of this size. And we circularized the whole country." Meaning that Prager's sent out flyers, catalogues, and salesmen. "Christmas started in August. There were no racks. Everything got shoved into that room. It was like a forest of trees. All the walls filled with trees and ornaments. Balls, Christmas balls. By the time Christmas came, you were so sick of it you didn't want to do it.

"We had big stores. Eaton's and The Bay. And mom-and-pop shops. City people know about us and they love to come. We used to have customers come in from Newfoundland and they would buy lots and lots and lots of stuff. And they were a lot of fun. In the olden days, we were open Saturdays and we'd put a sandwich board out. We once hired a guy in a sandwich board to walk up and down Spadina. [The public] could come in and buy trees and such."

My parents took me to Prager's when I was a kid. We bought a Barcana balsam. I remember the trip.

"Barcana was from someplace in Quebec. They used to make bendies — mannequins that bend. You want to put a mannequin on a bicycle — you know, in a sports good store. Noma went under the year before last. I don't know what happened to Barcana. They went under sometime before that. There's only one Canadian company still making trees."

"We manufacture thirty-two different styles of trees," Lisa Langelier tells me. Langelier's the office manager at MelMax Decorations Inc. of Cowansville, Quebec. "Every style of tree is available." White, black, copper, red, purple, blue. "Fashion colours," Langelier calls them.

MelMax started up in 1995, staffed by former Barcana employees. It specialized in wreaths, then branched out.

"We always want to have fun," Langelier says. "Challenge ourselves." MelMax has become a Christmas tree innovator. It makes upside-down Christmas trees, asymmetrical trees, tinsel trees in matte colours. Black trees for Halloween. "We're very lucky," Langelier says, "to have a team of people who share a common passion for Christmas.

"The machines we have on hand are designed and built in-house," Langelier says. "It enables us to increase our production capacity at any given time." A machine shreds strips of PVC. Another weaves it through the twisted wire branches. Staffers fluff needles. "Production runs from February right up until Christmas," Langelier says. The factory includes a showroom. It's open year-round.

Made in Canada. It's stamped across the MelMax catalogue. "The only raw material that is not local is the plastic PVC," Langelier says. "There's no company producing this film in Canada." The rest of the tree is native — the metal used in branches, the tubing used in trunks. "The hinges that hold the tree branches, the boxes, labels." Tree stands are made of wood.

TREES
$2

13

TREE STANDS

DAVID SHORT IS a designer of "medical, mainly rehab, devices," he says. "Physiotherapy machines for testing muscle strength."

He has his own company, Northwave Designworks in Kingston, Ontario. "If you ever used one of those computerized devices that you sit on and you crank against to measure your knee strength," he says, "I was involved in that kind of design."

I'm asking Short about another design he did. A non-medical design for a Christmas tree stand.

I discovered David Short at the Canadian Intellectual Property Office in Ottawa. Short wasn't there, but his design was. "Tree holder," it's called. He filed his patent application years ago. It takes years to process a patent in Canada.

"I had a number of Christmas trees fall down," Short says. "I tried different tree stands. The three-legged tree stands, and some plastic ones that were supposed to be better. I'd mount them on plywood. And everyone's tied their tree to the wall at some time. If I'm having problems with trees falling over, probably everyone else is," Short says. "The more people you talk to, the more that becomes apparent. I thought, 'I'm an engineer, I should be able to come up with something better than this.'"

"Christmas Tree Stand." Another patent in the Canadian Patent Office. It's the earliest Canadian patent for a tree stand, dated 1929.

How did Christmas trees stand before 1929? Not well. Trees tipped, overloaded with ornaments. And not just ornaments. In the nineteenth century, it was usual to string Christmas cards to trees. Santa stashed gifts — gifts wrapped in tissue — between branches, not beneath the tree. Some hung cornucopias containing candy, or hung stockings on trees. Some of those stockings were stuffed with coal or wood shavings — stockings for brats.

Families planted trees in pails of dirt, or in wooden soap crates weighted with wet sand. Some families stacked flatirons about the trunk. Some ran guywires from the four corners of the room to hold up the tree. I spoke to a woman whose father hung trees from the ceiling. Hung them so high she could walk underneath the trunks.

"Safety Xmas Tree Holder" was an item advertised in *Ladies Home Journal* in 1889. The first commercial tree stand, it looked like a stone jar. Bark and leaves grew in relief up the sides. A tree butt slipped into the top and three screws held the trunk secure. The tree stood up straight. "Several features are claimed for a new Christmas tree holder; steadiness and durability, it being possible to use it a second season."

This tree holder was cast-iron, as all early Christmas stands were. They weighed a ton. Just try toppling them. Some rotated — a concealed clockwork mechanism spun the tree. These came in two sizes: small for the home, larger models for hotels and churches. Hidden music-box mechanisms played Christmas carols. "Silent Night," then "O Come, Little Children."

A cast-iron tree stand could cost a man a week's wages. The poor stuck with pails. In the early 1900s, stores sold "block holders" for a quarter. Block holders were two wooden planks nailed into an X with a hole gouged in the centre where the tree trunk went. But block holders only held trunks of a certain size. And if fire broke out, they burned.

"It would take a blowtorch to maintain a fire in a freshly cut tree," says a tree-growing guide. Fresh trees take time to burn. Not so freshly cut trees? No time. A tree in a living room is basically tinder. Branches brown, become eminently burnable. "You can observe this by dropping a twig in your fireplace," warns *Canadian Consumer* magazine. "The resin in the needles and branches makes it highly inflammable. The drier the tree, the more hazardous."

In the 1920s, the Novelty Industry Company started selling tree stands cast in iron from their foundry in Brockville, Ontario. I own one — I bought it antiquing. It cost me a ton. In the 1920s, it cost a dollar. It's three-legged, like a flag stand. The trunk slots into a hole, sits in a bowl of water. A dead tree can drink a quart or so of water a day.

Tree stands with water bowls were the unheralded heroes of Christmas holidays. Well-watered trees are less likely to catch fire and slower to incinerate. The Novelty Industry Company didn't invent them. Many companies made them. Many families owned them and were safer for it.

By the Depression, steel versions of the stand were for sale. These were a tad tippier than cast iron stands. Then came tin holders. They needed to be nailed to the floor.

"I was always playing around with something better," David Short says. "I worked on hundreds of different designs, everything from U-bolt-type clamps to cables." After years of work, Short had it: the Bear Paw.

The Bear Paw holds more than six litres of water. "Most tree stands have these little thumbscrews that come in and try to clamp the tree," Short says. "Thing is, the tree trunk is probably not perfectly round. After a week or so, it's gotten pretty slippery, and the wood's started to deform a bit. It'll find its way out from among those little flimsy thumbscrews."

The Bear Paw has saw-toothed clamps that sink into the tree from every side. "They dig right into the tree with about 300 pounds of force." Short's sure his tree stand would be a sure seller if he could get backers onboard. "Problem is, everyone's looking for another Microsoft. Tell them you've got a better Christmas tree stand, they don't see the huge potential."

In 1992, Mike Bolster was working at a machine shop in Plaster Rock, New Brunswick. "I worked inside sales and learned a bit about custom fab, welding, machining, hydraulics, etc.," he says. The company also made Christmas tree stands.

"Their main business was servicing the logging industry and during the slow months they didn't want to lose their key workers." So the company put their crew to work on tree stands. "They would cut, weld and paint a thousand or so of these stands and then sell them around the Maritimes."

That Christmas, a Canadian Tire store in Moncton sold 100 of the stands. The retailer ordered 13,500 for the following year. Bolster's employers couldn't deliver, so Bolster stepped in, founding Christmas Mountains Manufacturing Inc. "I bought a bunch of used production-line equipment and built jigs and packing tables. My eighteen-year-old brother helped construct the factory. We had no plumbing or insulation. The toilet was a porta-potty."

Bolster, his brother, and twelve employees worked twelve-hour shifts. They filled all orders. Bolster redesigned the tree stand, adding a plastic liner where the water went, making the stands rust- and leak-proof. "Orders started coming in for 1994," he says. "I had 30,000 units sold, and was getting ready to start production, when a fire started in the shop. It was a total loss."

Bolster begged and borrowed money to rebuild. He bought an empty furniture store. "I slept only a few hours, on a couch left by the furniture dealer. We were able to produce 1,000 tree stands every nine hours. We actually turned our first profit."

Contracts came in from the United States, Singapore, China. Bolster continued to invent new products. His company now offers a range of tree stands. The largest handles twenty-footers. Bolster invented plastic hooks to attach Christmas wreaths to doors. No need to put nails in the woodwork anymore. He invented plastic trays to sit beneath trees, catching needles and water. He invented the "Auto Stop Watering System." The device slips into the reservoir of a tree stand. The tree owner pours water into a funnel; it runs through a plastic tube into the device. When the stand is full, the device cuts off water flow. "Never crawl on the floor or overfill your tree stand again," promises the watering system's catalogue blurb.

"It's a great way to prevent fire," Bolster says.

Bolster knows about fire.

A well-watered tree in a stable stand will still burn. Keep water fresh, and bleach the water bowl. Bacteria keep water from being sucked up into the tree. Some tree owners spike water with sugar, claiming it keeps needles greener. Do your needles look ill? Add aspirin.

Don't keep a dead tree in the house. Don't keep it in the garage. Shake off loose needles, make a potpourri. Burn the trunk, but remove ornaments first — fake snow and tinsel produce toxic smoke.

Canadian cities used to incinerate Christmas trees by the thousands. Trees full of sap take two hours to burn, leaving behind spiky stumps that jammed incinerators. Smoke choked city workers. Some

Canadian cities have experimented with wood chippers. Calgary started such a recycling program in the 1980s. It now chips 40,000 Christmas trees a year. It spreads the chips on park trails. Chips shield flower beds from frost.

Drag your tree outdoors. Hang suet from the branches, for birds. Sprinkle needles over azaleas. A suggestion from Christmas tree historian Phillip V. Snyder is to tie a tree to a brick or cement block, then toss it in a lake. Fish use trees as cover. Picture it: a forest of firs, afloat, uninflammable. Underwater. Fish silver as ornaments.

14

LIGHTS

1.

CHRISTMAS 1867. IT'S delightful. I'm at Black Creek Pioneer Village, a re-created country village in the suburbs of Toronto. An historical museum. Life here is as it was in nineteenth-century Ontario, or so says the brochure.

The sky looks like snow. Actors portray villagers. A schoolteacher lights candles in her classroom to illuminate the Christmas pageant. A minister lights candles in his church to illuminate Christmas services. Carollers carry candles to light their way at twilight.

"Everyone makes their own candles," Catherine Parr Traill wrote in *Backwoods of Canada* in 1836. Country-dwelling Canadians made candles by dipping wicks in fat, or by pouring fat into candle moulds.

Tallow, it's called. Fat from livestock. A single hog made a hundred candles. Parr Traill blended beef and pig fat to mould her candles. Tallow candles spat. Smelled like supper.

"CANDLES!" shouted an ad in an 1886 edition of the Montreal *Gazette*. A shop on Port Street carried stock shipped in from England. City dwellers bought commercial candles, which came in all shapes and for all purposes. Piano candles stood atop pianos. Boudoir candles came in pink. There were carriage candles for the carriage trade.

Commercial candles were made of paraffin. Club Sperm candles were made of sperm drawn from the head of the sperm whale. Wax myrtles flourish along the Atlantic coast. Their berries were boiled down, and wax was extracted. Clear wax, with a tinge of green. It burned without smoke, and smelled fruity when snuffed.

Candles crafted specifically for Christmas appeared in the 1890s. What made a regular candle Christmassy? The colour. Red or green. A store in Montreal advertised hand-painted Christmas candles. Lead paint? Let's hope not.

The earliest commercial Christmas candles were tapers and columns. Tapers were short, skinny candles to burn on nightstands and in wreaths. Columns were tall candles that burned at holiday dinners and receptions. Another staple shape was the short spiral. Cable candles, they were called. Cable candles aren't sold much anymore. They were used to decorate Christmas trees.

Cable candles sat on the tips of branches. The spiral design, it was said, kept candle drippings from hitting the needles. Many Canadians crafted their own tree candles. Stores sold moulds. Families melted down old candle butts and stubs.

The Copp Clark Company sold tree candles by the box. A box held forty-eight. Dime a dozen. In an issue of *Godey's* magazine from the 1860s, a woman wrote that it would "take a whole box of one hundred colored candles" to illuminate her tree to the desired degree.

"On Christmas night," wrote Clare McAllister, conjuring memories of a Victorian Christmas in British Columbia, "the candles would be lit, and there is nothing more magical than a living room fireplace blazing and the candles in a dim room on a lighted tree; it's a very magical thing."

Candles posed another problem: how to attach them to trees?

"A tree stood in the schoolhouse lighted with three inches of wax candle wedged in a hundred rifle cartridges tied to the branches," wrote Robert J. Renison, a settler who attended a nineteenth-century Christmas celebration at a schoolhouse in a town on James Bay.

Some dripped wax onto branches, then pressed candles into the wax, hoping they would remain standing. Some pinned candles to limbs. Stores started selling Christmas-tree candle holders at the turn of the twentieth century — clamps with tin teeth that bit into branches. Nippers, they were called. Counterweight candle holders balanced on branches. They resembled wishbones. Balls added weight to the ends. There were cups to catch wax drippings. Wax was a problem. It stained floors, clothes. Worse was fire.

"The installation of Christmas trees is a source of danger," a Québécois fire chief confirmed in the early 1920s. "Don't use candles. Use metallic instead of paper or cotton decorations." He warned against leaving children alone with trees. "Instruct each member of the family with the situation and operation of the nearest fire alarm box."

At this point, fire extinguishers hadn't been invented. Canadians didn't keep their tree candles lit for long — an hour a day, maybe. Sometimes only on Christmas Eve. Parents kept pails of dirt near their trees — dirt and well water.

Old rugs to smother sparks, sponges tied to broomsticks. None worked very well. A tree could burn in seconds, a room in minutes. "There have been scores of Christmas tree fatalities in homes and in Sunday schools," reported the Montreal *Gazette* in 1901.

Edward Johnson worked for Thomas Edison, who invented electric lamps in 1879. In 1882, Johnson hung his Christmas tree with a string of electric lamps, or "electric candles," as they were called.

"In the near future," wrote a columnist for a Canadian daily in 1882, "when electricity becomes a little cheaper, incandescent lights will make the tree a blaze of glory, and there will be no fear of a catastrophe."

Commercial Christmas-tree-light outfits went into production in the early 1900s. Filaments inserted into airless bulbs. They were pricey. A turn-of-the-century set could cost someone a month's wages. Department stores rented out lights to families.

"Unlike candles," writes Christmas historian Robert Brenner, "[early lighting outfits] could be turned on or off at random, could be painted in various colors, and were SAFE." Well, somewhat safe. The tips of some early Christmas lights were sharp enough to slice skin. The earliest bulbs also got hot enough to scorch skin, or trees.

At first, Canadians bought American Christmas lights, sets manufactured by General Electric in Schenectady, New York, or in New York City by the Henry W. McCandless Company.

By the 1920s, a company called Messervey Industries had begun making electric Christmas lights in their factory in Bridgeport, Ontario. By 1932, Noma — National Outfit Manufacturer's Association — had set up shop in Canada. Founded in 1925 when fifteen American Christmas-light manufacturers merged, the company opened a factory outside of Owen Sound, Ontario. In the States, their boxes bore images of Uncle Sam. In Canada, Santa Claus.

During the Depression, Noma experimented with Textolite, bulbs cast from fibreglass and resin, a mix that didn't melt or hit high temperatures. "Traditional candles," said *Chatelaine*, "are now replaced by small electric bulbs in actual candle form." Noma sold candle-shaped lights and electric candles that sat safely in wreaths and on mantels. Stores also sold counterfeit candles that clipped to Christmas trees — metal or glass or paper tubes with tinsel flames. Tinsel flames flickered in a draft.

Electricity rendered candles decorative. Stores sold them as such. "Recognizing the popular trend toward greater use of candles for decoration," said a trade magazine of the giftware industry in 1942, "the manufacturers have been paying more and more attention to the decorative lines."

Department and specialty stores set up "Candle Corners" at Christmastime. Christmas "is undoubtedly the time of greatest demand," wrote the trade magazine. Retailers convinced customers that Christmas was "incomplete without the splendor of lighted candles." Candles, stores said, were traditional, old-fashioned. Red, green, white. "Other colours to match their room decorations may also be used."

F. Baillargeon Limitée started creating candles in 1896. Its bread and butter: religious institutions. Baillargeon's factory in St. Catherine, Quebec, produced different makes for different rites. Liturgical lamps had to burn for up to fourteen days. Easter candles often stood five feet tall.

By the 1930s, churches in cities and countries had converted to electricity. Churches still used candles, but not as many as before. F. Baillargeon introduced a new line: domestic candles, "for every purpose," according to a company ad. "Anniversaries, Receptions, Weddings, Banquets." And there were other — more puzzling — purposes for candles: "Flower Bowls, Cake Sets, Florists, Dinners."

"The hostess's problem to create a distinctive and congenial atmosphere is greatly simplified when she utilizes the light of candles," suggested Baillargeon. "Used correctly, candles enhance her reputation for taste and good judgement."

To stiffen them, Baillargeon workers dipped wicks in wax baths. Wicks were then attached to a Ferris-wheel-type apparatus. The wheel turned. At the bottom the wicks entered a vat of dripless, odourless paraffin. Twenty-four to twenty-six turns later, the wheel stopped, white tapers hanging off. Chandlers added stearin to the paraffin, for opacity.

For moulded candles, Baillargeon used moulding machines. In the 1940s, novelty candles hit stores. Star shapes. Snowball shapes. Cherubs and chubby Santas and snowmen on skates. "They're Christmas candles," said an ad for Eaton's. "A lovable refreshing collection of candles that are sure to find themselves playing an important part in your Christmas decorating plans!" Eaton's in Winnipeg stocked them at their surgical counter.

If the ads are any indication, the most common novelty candle was the Christmas tree. A tree that was safe to burn.

2.

My dad called them "strings." Springs and summers, strings sat in a box in the basement. Autumns he untangled them, laid them out on the lawn, then plugged them in. Nothing. His strings were wired in series: if one light died, the whole string died. Bulbs always burned out.

Dad affixed lights to eaves, stapled them up porch posts. He outlined windows in red and green. A connect-the-dot house.

Festoons. The correct name for a string of Christmas lights. Indoor electric Christmas outfits appeared in the 1880s. Outdoor outfits came a little later. They burned hot, shattered during cold snaps. By the 1920s, they'd improved. There were thicker cables, thicker insulation. Paint was now applied on the insides of the bulbs.

Canadians didn't seem to know what to do with outdoor outfits. In 1932, the *Winnipeg Free Press* published hints for those who were "a bit hazy" about decorating with lights. Suggestions included "colored lights placed in trees and shrubbery; strings of colored lights draped around verandahs; flower boxes decorated with lights."

The 1930s. Outdoor lighting, said Winnipeg's mayor, Lieutenant-Colonel Ralph Humphreys Webb, "will give us all an opportunity of sharing our happiness with others who are not quite so fortunate."

"But the most exciting Christmas decorations follow the modern trend for out-door decorations," said a pamphlet, *Decorating with*

Color-Light, put out by the Noma Electric Company in the 1930s. The pamphlet contained step-by-step instructions for silhouetting a house with Christmas lights. "Christmas colors turn holiday nights into magic." Outline decorating, it was called. Noma sold set of lights packed with packets of staples. Bestselling shades were red, blue, then green. Pink was also popular.

My grandfather hung lights on his eaves, an upside-down chevron of yellow and blue. On his roof, he had a Santa jigsawed from wood, then painted. In Santa's hands, reins — a festoon of Christmas lights lashed to Dasher, Dancer, Prancer, Vixen. Wooden reindeer. My grandfather made them with woodworking patterns he ordered from a company in California. I'm not sure what happened to the rest of Santa's team. Termites?

"So join the fun," recommended *Popular Mechanics* in 1951, "and 'outshine' your neighbors on Christmas Eve." Their article offered carpentry instructions for constructing snowmen, angels, and stars to star on rooftops and in yards.

Do-it-yourself props were all the rage. Shadow boxes containing crèches. Angels heralding whomever came down the drive. "Candles also can be improvised by covering a wooden frame or half of a cardboard rug-shipping tube with translucent plastic or oilcloth, using a spotlight at the base or a string of lights inside the tube."

Noma noticed the trend toward props, and became the first Canadian company to manufacture commercial Christmas props. In 1957, Noma offered "a natural rounded complete figure of the beloved Santa" for the first time. He stood like a streetwalker, a 15-watt red lamp burning inside him. "Light penetration both front and back," boasted Noma's catalogue. "He will sell himself."

Noma's other figures were flat-backed. Vinylite carollers, candles, reindeer. A Vinylite Nativity, a "faithful reproduction of Christmas manger scene." Pink vinyl trees — plant them in yards. A four-foot vinyl tree rigged with 60- and 40-watt lamps. This was sold with the proviso: "EXTREMELY COLORFUL AND SHOWY."

Noma also sold metal lamppost brackets, so that the figures could be fixed to posts, fences, trees. A strong wind and a flat-backed reindeer flies.

A trio of choirboys, twenty feet in the air. They stood silhouetted by pipe organs and white candles, a fifty-foot tree beside them.

"We get hundreds of letters every year about our display," said A. C. Olmstead. "It's very good business." Olmstead worked for

G. H. Wood and Company industrial sanitation engineers. Starting at Christmas 1952, G. H. Wood installed thousands of lights and props around their property. It caught on. Hundreds of cars drove down Toronto's Queen Elizabeth Way to see them.

The company's neighbours noticed. In 1955, Molson's lit their brewery. Loblaw Groceterias illuminated a giant tree the following year, as did Shell Oil. Shopping malls installed millions of lights a year in the 1950s, as did churches. "The more lights there are the better I like it," Dr. E. M. Howse of the United Church of Canada told the *Financial Post* in 1964.

Noma established Noma Displays, Ltd. Lighting men submitted sketches to businesses in the spring or summer. Contracts were signed in October. In November, display men installed the displays. Giant candles, thirty-foot trees that towered on pipes over business. In January, Noma dismantled the designs, then stored them, for a fee.

"Industries," commented the *Financial Post*, "like homeowners, follow the old pattern of 'keeping up with the Joneses.'"

"It is understood that several American cities decorate quite extensively for the Christmas period," Vancouver's city clerk wrote to the mayor in 1947. "Therefore, to assist the Electrician in advising respecting a policy in this regard, it is felt that he should be authorized to visit cities as far south as Portland and enquire regarding schemes in operation of these cities."

Vancouver became one of the first Canadian cities with a coherent decorating scheme. The city convened a special committee for "Decorative Christmas Lighting." The committee established a "standard of Christmas lighting." Business districts submitted decorating plans to the committee. The committee okayed them. It purchased lights and ornaments, many of them from Noma, then rented them out for a fee. It negotiated insurance rates. It paid the electricity bill.

In 1957, the committee rented out six balls of tarred marlin, seven pounds of hog rings, and 3,000 feet of cedar rope. In later years, the Hastings Chamber of Commerce hired a radio station to broadcast Christmas tunes nonstop. Concealed crystal-controlled radio tuners along Hastings Street picked up the music and blasted it to pedestrians. The Fraser District Business Association erected a Santa Castle in an empty lot.

Red, green, yellow, copper — the most popular colours of public light displays. Colours that can be seen across distances. Purples tend to disappear.

"My name's Jerry MacDonald. I have this nickname: instead of saying 'Merry Christmas' they say, 'There's Jerry Christmas.'" MacDonald's an assistant superintendent with the city of Charlottetown, Prince Edward Island. "If there's anything to do with Christmas in the city of Charlottetown, I'm the one they call.

"I've been working at this Christmas stuff for a good twenty-five years. When we started out, we did the old downtown city. We probably only had ten Christmas trees, we'd decorate City Hall with a few things. Now, we decorate City Hall, municipal buildings, anything that we can light up in business areas out in Sherwood or Parkdale."

Charlottetown founded Wintertide, its festival of lights, in the 1990s. It illuminates the city in December. "For Wintertide alone, without Christmas trees and buildings or anything, I'll buy 72,000 bulbs," MacDonald says. "A crew goes in there a week before putting them up and puts a new bulb in every one of them. It's all done in a professional way. I've got teams out there checking everything from bulbs to trees that are crooked. They just have a duty to do, and that's what they do all day long for an eight-hour day."

Props, too, are part of MacDonald's responsibilities. "I've put in two globes with 'Peace on Earth' — it's bilingual, 'Peace on Earth' — which stand probably thirty feet. They're out in Victoria Park. We have a big City of Charlottetown sign coming in off the bridge in Stratford. So we put Santa Claus with presents up there. And they had planted probably sixty little tiny spruce trees and I lit them with minilights. We do a New Year's Eve in the park for the families. I light a trail up for the children and I have all these little houses and they look like real houses. I have a sign that says, 'Magical Trail.'"

MacDonald buys Asian-made bulbs, props from the United States. Alderbrook Industries bought Noma's Christmas division in 1997. Alderbrook declared bankruptcy in 2002, unable to compete with cheap ornaments from Asia and America.

"We always did lights at Christmas when I was growing up," MacDonald says. "I can remember helping Dad put the lights on the house, candles in the window. With house lights these days, you'll get areas of town that really go to town and look really nice. And there's not as much in other areas. You can see some people getting into it. It seems with the city, the more we decorate, we see more houses and that getting into it."

Does he get into it at home?

"It's funny. I was with my fiancée a week ago and we were doing it. I decorate the whole city, but when it comes to decorating the house, I just do what she tells me. I learned my lesson. I say, 'Yes, dear, whatever you like.' And it looks good, too."

15

REINDEER

HOW TO MAKE *mouffle*: shoot a moose; cut off the nose; place it in hot coals. The hair burns off. Be sure to burn the nostril hairs, too. The nose turns white. Ligaments scrape off. Boil the meat with onions and vegetables, to taste.

"The calf is very small, and is taken from the cow by the Caesarean operation long before it attains its full growth. This, boiled whole, is one of the most esteemed dishes amongst the epicures of the interior."

That's boiled buffalo baby, a Christmas treat at Fort Edmonton in 1847. But hardly the only meat on the table. A priest, it is said, passed around buffalo tongue.

But the ultimate Canadian Christmas feast is beaver: "Remove the beaver tail from the body of the animal. Dip it into boiling water to remove the outer skin, exposing the meat.

"To cook in a stone oven, place on a rack over a drip pan. To cook over an open fire, skewer the tail on a green stick and cook slowly over coals. This meat is very fat and rich and must be allowed to drip. Save the drippings to use over potatoes baked in their skins in an oven or campfire."

Canada's earliest Christmas parades starred dinner, not Santa.

"Several hundred people paraded . . . having in their midst a sleigh on which was placed a frozen porker." So said the Montreal *Gazette* in 1867. The sleigh proceeded up Rue Saint-Roch — a Christmas vision. "The animal was gorgeous," the paper wrote, "decked with chaplets of evergreens around his neck, and to its tail was attached a piece of crape [sic]."

Abattoirs sleighed holiday meats through streets. Cuts on cutters — mutton, caribou, venison. Bears fattened for the holidays. Carcasses covered with snow-white cloths, to keep them clean. "The procession had many admirers among the great throngs of Christmas shoppers on the streets," wrote a Prairie paper of one such parade. "It is questionable if the famed cornbelt could produce anything of finer quality."

Meat parades wound down at market halls. "It was difficult to move around in the building," wrote a reporter in the *Manitoba Daily Free Press* in 1882, "on account of the piles of carcasses lying around await-ing their turn to be suspended in graceful positions to contribute to the general adornment."

Butchers bedecked stalls with boughs of evergreens. Sprigs of holly stuck from sides of meat, as did miniature flags, paper cards bearing mottoes, and bows tied about T-bones.

Butchers sawed horns from elks and attached them to steers. Bears sported deer racks. One Prairie paper reported seeing the head and horns of a moose neatly stitched to the body of a cow. "A few jokes are being perpetrated," acknowledged the *Free Press* reporter in 1882, "among which may be mentioned the sorriest looking specimen ever seen of the carcass of a sheep, there being only skin and bones observable."

In *The Book of Small*, Emily Carr recalls a Victoria butcher shop at Christmas: "Naked sheep had bunches of coloured paper where their heads ought to have been and flowers and squiggles carved in the fat of their backs." In the late nineteenth century, it was common to carve holiday designs — stars, holly, mottoes — into carcasses. Some motifs were painted onto meat; others were powdered onto it. There were also butchers who refused to do this, fearing it affected the taste.

Days before the holidays, butchers slaughtered their best Christmas beef on the floors of markets. In 1906, a Winnipeg butcher killed a cow called Jumbo. Jumbo weighed 2,200 pounds alive, 1,600 pounds dressed out. Also killed: Prince Charlie and Happy Jim. Crowds collected. Cheered.

By the 1920s, Christmas caribou was scarce. Labrador still had herds. Northwest Canada did not. "Where were the caribou, which used to darken the endless plains?" asked one reporter. "Suddenly, their haunts knew them no more."

Caribou migration patterns had shifted. Caribou had been over-hunted by white settlers, trappers, prospectors. Inuvialuit had for eons killed caribou with bows and arrows. Then they got hold of guns, which killed them quicker.

Not just caribou. Seals, walruses, bears, muskox — Arctic animals were vanishing. Inuvialuit were starving. Inuvialuit ate caribou meat, drank caribou milk. Sewed skins into coats and shoes and tents.

The Canadian government decided to do something about this. It called the American government. Alaskan Inuit had faced similar starvation decades before. The U.S. government had shipped reindeer in from Siberia. Reindeer are a kind of caribou — the domesticated kind. The Americans' goal was to teach Inuit how to ranch reindeer, in hopes they could use them to feed themselves. In hopes that they could market reindeer meat to meat eaters across America.

The Canadian government followed suit. In 1929, it contracted an American company to drive thousands of reindeer from Siberia into northwestern Canada. On Christmas Day 1929, a herd set out from Nabaktoolit, near Nome. Over 2,000 miles to go, across muskeg, mountains. A pair of Dutch botanists led the drive, assisted by a reindeer herder from Lapland and his small black-and-white dogs. Reindeer dogs. Lapp dogs.

A blizzard hit. Then another, and another. In snow, reindeer turn their heads to keep snowflakes from flying up their noses. A thousand deer strayed away. In Howard Pass, a hurricane hit; reindeer died. In spring they fawned. Wolves attacked the fawns. A pack could take down as many as fifty a night. Herders attacked wolves on skis, which let them move quicker than their quarry. Which they then clubbed.

Mosquitoes. Blackflies. Bulldogs, a variety of blackfly, bit their way under reindeer skin, ruining hides and starting stampedes. Deer would race into the wind to try to lose them — whichever way the wind was blowing. The reindeer hurt themselves charging into spruce forests. Antlers were entangled in branches. Deer hanged themselves.

It was supposed to take two years. In 1935, three thousand reindeer straggled into the Mackenzie Grazing Reserve on the east side of the Mackenzie River Delta. Most of the original herd had died. Their offspring finished the trip. Their new home: thousands of acres near the Bering Strait. The government divided the herd into smaller herds which would be the wards of Inuvialuit herders.

The Inuvialuit herders and their families were due to sail in. They never arrived: their ship sunk in a storm, all lost. Other Inuvialuit families took control of the herds, tending them on twenty-hour shifts. Day and night, in heat and cold. The meat made them little money. Again herds collapsed.

The Canadian government tried a different tack. They forgot about feeding the Inuvialuit. Some reindeer they sold, some they put in the care of a private contractor. The contractor modernized, introducing aircraft for reconnaissance, radios for herdsmen. He built an abattoir.

Roasts, steaks, chops, ribs. Reindeer meat hit stores. Jerky proved popular at taverns. Reindeer sausages didn't find much of a market. Reindeer meat was canned and labelled Eskimo Food.

Reindeer skins became coats. Antlers sold as gun racks. Artisans carved antlers into knife handles. Velvet scraped from antlers was sold to the Chinese, who sold it as an aphrodisiac. Offal could be cooked into food for herders' dogs. Reindeer fat yields stearic acid.

According to a report from the Department of Indian Affairs and Northern Development in 1967, "There is also a market for live reindeer to be used in promotions which involve a Christmas theme and Santa Claus."

Dawn Abel grew up in Vancouver in the 1960s. She remembers the reindeer. "They weren't actually in Woodward's. They were in a building out in the parking lot. It was where they used to take groceries. They'd take them out with your number on it, and when you were done shopping, you'd drive your car up there, give them your number and you'd get your groceries."

At Christmas, reindeer came to Woodward's Department Store. "They had them in a shed. All we could see was their heads and stuff. So we could reach out and touch their noses. But we were protected from their feet." Reindeer's forelegs kick forward.

"I remember the awe of seeing these magnificent animals with these big horns. It was the highlight of Christmas. It was a big part of my childhood. And going to see Santa," she adds. Abel's not sure where the reindeer came from. A local zoo? A reindeer farm?

The Peace River runs through northern British Columbia. Peace River is a town on the Peace River. By 1989, Abel had settled outside of town with her husband and her kids.

"My father got us interested," she says. "He heard that they needed to move reindeer out of the Northwest Territories. Because of some dispute up there, they were going to sell the reindeer off." Abel and some neighbours formed the Peace Country Reindeer Association. The Association paid to have two rail-liner loads of reindeer delivered. The liners took three days to arrive.

ReputAbel Farm: that's what they called it. Reindeer grazed on twenty-five acres. Tundra, with some trees to shield them from sun. The Abels breed deer. They started with ten; today they have fifty. They sell deer to other farmers, who start their own herds. They sell deer for meat.

Dawn Abel keeps a few deer on a five-acre plot near her house. These are the deer she's training to star in show business.

"The U.S. companies come into Canada and choose Vancouver," Abel says. "There's actually a digest put out of the animal actor agencies. So the movie company goes to the animal actor agency and says, 'This is what we need.' Then the company goes about finding the animals if they don't have them themselves."

Abel's been contracted for television commercials and television movies. Her biggest shoot was the 2003 feature film *Elf*. "We spent several months training here on the farm," she says. "Training involves getting them used to us, getting them used to being restrained on a halter, and then, used to us being around them. Then they had to learn to stand with their harness hooked into a sleigh set-up. And stand there and behave. It was a lot of work."

Abel put eight trained reindeer in a trailer and transported them to Vancouver. *Elf*'s producers provided a large grassy pen.

"It was night shoots, so it wasn't a lot of fun. We mostly hung out in the pen during the night. We didn't talk to anybody we weren't supposed to in the chain of command. You sit and you wait and you wait and you wait. The first night it rained. We were soaking wet. The next few nights were cold; there was ice on their water trough. Our food was great. Awesome caterers."

Some reindeer farmers stage Christmas shows. "We have talked about setting up a Christmas display and having people come out and having pictures taken," Abel says. "It would be a lot of work for the little amount of money you would make."

Abel focuses her efforts on public appearances. "I have to stay active with them. It takes a lot of work for one or two shows a year. You have to talk to them and reassure them and make sure there's no running or loud noises going on around them. We're one of the only ones doing this in B.C. There is one guy down in Mission that has one deer."

The reindeer have been all over, she says. Fall fairs, Santa Claus parades. "They've been on location at the Garden City Shopping Centre down in Richmond. Kids love them. We ended up having a security guard at the gate. Parents thought they could just open the gate and send their children in. Children would come running at them. The deer were beside themselves. Their first thought is to flee. They're flight animals."

"But they don't really fly," I say.

"They've been on Grouse Mountain. Up on the top of Grouse they have a skating rink, and a big lodge with a big ski hill. Kids would go in to see Santa, then they'd see the reindeer. It was all part of the show. The reindeer rode on the gondola up to the top. Walked on, rode up, hung out while the kids came. They had a fence there. They enjoyed it."

16

DINNER

"CHRISTMAS PUDDING PREPARED BY TONS." In 1923, the Canadian National Railways served two tons of plum pudding to guests on their dining cars. Many more tons went to patrons of the CNR's hotel restaurants.

"This Christmas pudding is made from an old English recipe," said an article in the Montreal *Gazette*. Raisins, currants, sugar. Freight cars of chopped suet. The pudding did not include rum or brandy, "because the laws of the majority of provinces prohibit its use." Chefs in every city made it from scratch. Not only plum pudding, but mincemeat, thousands of servings of it. "The chief items on any Christmas dinner bill of fare" included puddings.

And turkeys. With cranberry sauce.

I.

Cranberries grow wild. In bogs. With peaty soil. Plenty of water. Almost every province has a wild cranberry bog.

Nova Scotia has many. Cranberries abound in the Annapolis Valley. The Mi'kmaq picked them — used them to make pemmican. Crushed the berries into dye for rugs, blankets, and porcupine quills. Settlers combed the bogs. What they didn't eat, they sold. Barrels of cranberries sat in general stores, fermenting.

In 1872, William McNeil planted cranberries at the edge of a peat bog on his property in Melvern Square. The first Canadian to cultivate cranberries. Within a decade, a clutch of cranberry farmers were working the Valley. They cut wild vines and planted them. Some imported vines from the United States. Early Black — that was one variety.

Americans had been cultivating cranberries for years, from Massachusetts to Wisconsin. A cranberry trade organization — the American Cranberry Exchange — mailed cranberry recipe booklets to Canadian consumers. It also ran ads: "Cranberry Sauce served with beef gives zest to the whole meal." Canadian stores stocked Cape Cod cranberries.

"In the year 1892, the cranberry growers sent their first carload over the Windsor & Annapolis R.R. to Montreal," announced the Annual Report of the Nova Scotia Fruit Growers' Association. These were the first cranberries to leave Nova Scotia. Another shipment of fifty barrels sailed via steamship to England. The Fruit Growers Association reported: "As yet, the English people are not accustomed to using cranberries; but with the present efforts that are being made to introduce their use there, we hope they will, before very long, have acquired the taste for our sauce."

As the nineteenth century closed, close to thirty Nova Scotian families farmed cranberries. John Latimer drained twenty acres of land. He planted two with Cape Cod vines. The Duke of York Cranberry Meadow, it was called. It's still around — Latimer's relatives run it.

"Of all the branches of agriculture," said the report, "none was so profitable."

Cranberries thrive near water. Nova Scotian farmers cleared lots beside streams, swamps, the sea. Cranberries thrive on damp soil — muck. Farmers dug ditches, the deeper the better. The water table just below. The muck they coated in a thin layer of sand, to retain the sun's heat.

They planted vines, which crept along the ditches. Creeping habit, it's called. Farmers warred with worms. By burying bugs in sand. When this didn't work, they sprayed the berries with a mix of lime and water and fish-oil soap. Fish-oil soap's never scarce in the Maritimes.

Frost hurt. Farmers flooded the ditches to protect the vines. They handpicked berries before winter frosts set in, sorting them in frost-proof sheds. Then they flooded the ditches again, washing away cuttings and fallen fruit. Miles of matted vines remained. The ditches stayed flooded over winter, icing over. Kids could skate on them.

The harvested cranberries had to be kept cold, but not too cold. Americans had experimented with storing cranberries. They sank boxes of berries in cold streams. The cranberries kept cold. And got mushy. Mushy berries don't sell. Berries were kept in barrels of cold water. The berries took on the taste of the wood. An American developed a misting system. It involved pouring a stream of water down onto an electric fan. But it misted unevenly. And it posed a shock threat.

Canadians kept berries in cold cellars and ice sheds. They shipped berries to general stores and groceterias, where they became the stores' problem. Berries softened in hot shops. Sterile rot set in. Cranberries are plum targets for a host of rots — early rot, blotch rot, end rot. Shoppers settled for bruised, bad berries, suitable for stewing, but not much else.

Herbert Oyler cultivated cranberries. In 1932, Oyler decided to do something different with his berries. He decided to "do them up." Oyler canned cranberry sauce. He wasn't alone. In 1940, Herbert and Viola Large of Malagash Station Road started Malagash Canners. Viola illustrated the labels. Rolph Clark Stone printed them. The Larges didn't farm cranberries, they bought them from local farms.

Oyler grew his goods, Early Blacks and Howes, on almost 100 acres of bogs in Kings County and Yarmouth County. The province's largest supplier in the 1940s, he imported machines from the States that cleaned cranberries, cut off their stems, and cooked them. He opened a canning factory, a barn-like building near Auburn. In summer, thirty-five Nova Scotians worked there. In fall, they picked; in winter, they canned. Oyler Brand Cranberry Sauce. As orders grew, he brought in berries from Quebec, New Brunswick. Wild berries from Prince Edward Island. Besides berries, he processed apples, pickles. He canned blueberries for pie-making.

Oyler was also the first to ship his cans out of province. He put up twenty-odd cans an hour. He didn't only use tin cans: he also used glass jars. He felt they sold better. They couldn't have been sold much better. Grocery stores snatched them up, as did railway dining cars and hotels. Oyler's factory soon supplied 99 percent of Canada's Christmas canned cranberry sauce. A Montreal cannery provided the rest.

During wartime, glass jars were hard to get. But Oyler found them. He had contacts. The military bought his cranberries and served them to soldiers overseas. The military supplied the jars.

Oyler's plant shut down in the seventies. The industry had moved to coastal British Columbia, where frost's rarely a worry. British Columbia's got hundreds of acres of cranberry bogs. The farms are giant, and under contract to soft drink corporations. The soft drink corporations also make cranberry juice.

Juice drives the contemporary cranberry industry, ever since doctors decided cranberry juice helps prevent urinary tract infections. Canadians drink cranberry juice for its vitamins. Canadians mix it in cocktails.

2.

"There was a turkey shoot," reported a Prairie newspaper in the winter of 1878, "at which quite a number of shots congregated."

Turkey shoots took place in gravel pits or clearings. Birds sat in barrels, shooters paid for shots. What they shot, they won. Shoots were popular events at armouries. For soldiers, it was target practice.

Not all shooters were sharpshooters. As the Prairie paper put it,

"One turkey stood fire for eighteen shots unscathed, and then in sheer disgust froze to death."

"Canada raises its own turkeys," reported a turn-of-the-century newspaper, "most of them coming from the Western plains where prairie housewives raise them." Turkeys were a cottage industry in the years following Confederation. Family farmers farmed them on a small scale. Some to eat, some to sell. Some to shoot in turkey shoots

Country stores took turkeys as trade. City markets took them on consignment. Butchers slit the birds' necks, hung them upside-down from hooks. A bled turkey was known as a "dressed" turkey. Butchers displayed barrels full of them come Christmas.

Grade A, Grade B, Grade C — letter grading hadn't been invented yet. Customers gutted their own birds. Where did a turkey come from? What had it been fed? Customers never knew. How to tell a quality turkey? Folk wisdom dictated that buyers "Look for shiny feathers. A quality bird will shine."

Fields. Rock. Lakes. The makeup of Manitoulin Island. Manitoulin Island sits in Lake Huron, and is the world's largest freshwater island.

Sheep and cows. Livestock grazed what grazable land there was. Wolves posed a problem, but at least they could be trapped. In 1890, grasshoppers swarmed Manitoulin Island, eating everything. The sheep starved.

A. J. Wagg Sr. imported turkeys — Manitoulin's first. Wagg had heard that turkeys ate grasshoppers, which they do. His turkeys thrived, got fat. After a year, he had more than he needed. He sold some back to the mainland. Other islanders imitated Wagg. By 1895, Manitoulin Island had a new industry.

And the grasshoppers? Gone.

"Of all poultry," said the Montreal *Gazette* in 1903, "turkey is the hardest to rear." Manitoulin turkey farmers crammed their birds into sheds. In summer, the sheds cooked. In winter, they froze. Wood-burning stoves helped little. Turkeys are sensitive. If they get too cold, their wattles freeze.

Turkeys caught colds. Sinusitis could kill. This was before antibiotics were available, so farmers spiced wheat with licorice or ginger or red pepper. When fowl came down with blackhead — another name for enterohepatitis — farmers mixed arsenic into the feed. Enough to kill the bug, they hoped, but not enough to kill the bird.

Scientists stepped in. The Dominion government established a bureau on Manitoulin Island. The bureau taught farmers to keep turkeys out of manure. Manure carried tuberculosis. Concrete floors kept turkey talons clean. The bureau taught farmers about diet. Milk and roasted potatoes were good for fattening turkeys. Good for fattening anyone.

Before Christmas, Wagg and his fellow farmers drove turkeys to the island's North Shore on foot. If night fell during the trip, the turkeys roosted in trees.

Steamships put turkeys in pens and transported them to packing houses. The shipping route — across Georgian Bay, through the North Channel, onto Lake Superior — became known as the "Turkey Trail." In later years, a railway reached the island via a swinging bridge. A. J. Wagg constructed boxcars — cars with no walls. In summer, turkeys kept cool while travelling. In winter, canvas curtains shielded them.

Packing houses bled the birds, wrapped their heads in brown parcel paper. "New York Dressed," this was called. Pickers picked birds free of feathers. A good picker could pick up to sixty birds a day. Tail feathers went to factories, where they turned into feather dusters. Wings were sold as fans. Quills got ground into a pulp used to make artificial whalebone.

"Setting a good example to harassed Canadian housewives," reported the Canadian Press in 1931, "Canadian National Railways chefs have done their Christmas shopping early." To feed thousands of diners in dining cars and hotels, CNR chefs prepared 2,000 pounds of cranberries and 10,000 pounds of turkey. A thousand birds, the bulk of them from Manitoulin Island.

Simpson's roasted Manitoulin turkeys for their department store dining rooms. In Toronto, Eaton's home-delivered Christmas dinner on December 24. It included stuffing, sauce, sides, dessert, and a Manitoulin turkey. Servings for six, at a cost of three dollars.

In 1958, an eviscerating plant opened on Manitoulin Island in the town of Gore Bay. The plant bled birds, gutted them, wrapped the heads in parcel paper. Birds shipped out on ice. They reached the market mangled, skin soggy.

Loblaws didn't want soggy turkeys, so they transported live Manitoulin turkeys to a plant in Port Dover. The plant bled and gutted the birds, froze them in icy water, then sealed them in bags made of Cryovac, a film that shrunk when heated. Sealing the bird in a second skin.

Cryovac changed everything. Before its invention, turkeys had been wrapped in cellophane. Cellophane was loose. Iceboxes burned birds. Plants in Alberta and Manitoba started to offer fowl fully dressed — no heads, feet, or feathers. Another option: oven-ready, meaning the bird had been washed, pinned, and prestuffed. It was more expensive. It was most popular.

The Manitoba plant processed 30,000 a week. Superfarms supplied them, rearing hundreds of thousands of birds. Farmers learned how to speed turkey-egg production. Keep lights on in sheds all night. Feed turkeys steroids. Turkeys became available in two main sizes: family and hotel. Hotel turkeys were over eighteen pounds. The Poultry Products Institute of Canada campaigned to make turkey a weekly event. Newspaper ads, radio spots, displays — all proclaimed: EAT MORE TURKEY!

Manitoulin Island didn't have space for superfarms. Transportation to and from the island was time-consuming. The island's turkey farms died out. The eviscerating plant? Eviscerated.

"There is no longer a turkey plant in Gore Bay," says Annette Clarke. She's clerk of the town of Gore Bay. "To my knowledge, there are no turkey farmers, either. Some of the local farmers do raise and sell turkeys. But not in large quantities."

17

TRAINS

IN 1880, A toy train was news. In Manitoba. "In Donaldson's window may be seen a miniature railway," wrote the *Manitoba Daily Free Press* in December of 1880. Donaldson's was a Winnipeg dry-goods store. The train contained clockwork. Wind it up, and it rolled "gracefully and with alacrity. . . . No barbed wire fencing is needed to keep cows off the track."

Wind-up trains popped up in stores around the time of Confederation, as did "dribblers." Dribblers had engines. Boilers for water, alcohol lamps to boil the water. Steam pressure propelled the railway. Steam shot out of the smokestack.

And dribbled out the sides. Dribblers were sheet steel. Steel stamped into train shapes, folded, then soldered. But not well. Liquids leaked, tin melted. Sometimes the alcohol exploded. Manufacturers didn't mention this to kids.

Scientific American advertised an electric train in 1897. Few households had electricity at this time. The juice came from batteries. Wet batteries, with sulphuric acid as an ingredient. Railway manuals warned railroaders not to mix water in with the acid, or the acid would spit, burning surfaces and skin. Dry-cell batteries were safer. Toy-train historians Gerry and Janet Souter say each dry battery was "the size of a small artillery shell." They towered like grain silos over the trains.

Dust settles on soldiers. Moths terrorize teddy bears. Dolls with blinking eyes stare, unblinking. A toy train goes nowhere. A toy-shop window in Manhattan. The city's wired, the window isn't. Joshua Cowen stops to look. Doesn't like what he sees.

Cowen was an inventor. He'd invented the electric doorbell. In 1901, Cowen invented a train: "miniature electric cars with full accessories for window display and holiday gifts." Cowen's secret: a transformer, a coil of wires that stored electricity siphoned off from outlets and lamp sockets. He sold these along with his trains. The Lionel Train Company — that's what he called his company.

Lionel transformers transformed toy railways. They were cheap, and safe — relatively. They tended to heat up. Lionel encouraged operators to wear gauntlet gloves, just like real railroad engineers. Operators obliged.

Come Christmastime, Eaton's stores advertised Mechanical Halls. "All around are engines, motor cars, wagons, aeroplanes and many other mechanical toys." Trains took centre stage. Electric trains. Store decorators set up elaborate displays. "MECHANICAL TRAINS RUN ROUND A TRACK IN TOYLAND," ran a headline from a newspaper ad. Kids built toy bridges, elevators, automobiles, competing for cash prizes. "You should see the interest the boys take." Girls weren't interested in trains. Allegedly. Girls got another attraction — the Dolls' Palace.

Eaton's moved a lot of Lionel trains, and American Flyers, and Marx trains. Eaton's sold miniature models of Canadian Pacific Railway trains. "There's a mechanical streamlined engine, tender, four cars named Toronto, Winnipeg, Calgary, Vancouver, Montreal, Quebec — play you are conductor as well as owner and call out the stops." Models made in the United States, by Lionel.

Come Christmas, Eaton's installed them in stores in Montreal, Toronto, and Winnipeg — kiddie trains, the kind kids ride at carnivals. Kids paid a pittance — a nickel, a dime — and departed toy departments.

Eaton's installed the first Toyland train in Montreal in 1936. The train chugged through storerooms and canvas tunnels made up like Mother Goose Land. Little Boy Blue was there, a mannequin. Little Red Riding Hood — no wolf.

Decorators redid the décor yearly. Eaton's in Winnipeg offered "A Trip Across the North Pole." The train traversed an arctic ocean in blue fabric. A whale surfaced — it was cardboard. Balloons floated up from its blowhole. A plush penguin stood on the whale. Robot "Eskimo toddlers" cavorted with robot polar bear cubs and robot rabbits under a midnight sun.

Montreal's train travelled through a Giant's Cave: "Such thrills! Such wonders! Such things to see! Huge trees! A Great Big Giant!" Toronto's Toyland train travelled through a Christmas Fairyland, flying past elves at work making toys. At play, dancing in circles. Some elves just twitched erratically, shorting out.

Canadian National Railways manufactured Eaton's Toronto train. The engine was a replica of CNR locomotive number 6400. Four coaches carried twenty-four passengers at four miles per hour.

The other Toyland trains came courtesy of the Canadian Pacific Railway, the Montreal model a slick silver and black. The midget "3000," it was called, a sixth the size of the actual train. Angus Shops in Montreal built it, complete with air whistle, headlights, dynamos. Angus also built the Winnipeg train — twenty-five men worked on it, supervised by CPR's assistant to the chief engineer. The locomotive — a miniature version of a Royal Hudson — weighed 1,400 pounds. Cast-iron wheels, wood chassis, seats of red plush. For realism, the store poured crushed rock between the rails. Level-crossing gates lowered when the train passed.

After its annual Winnipeg stint, Eaton's packed up the train and shipped it — by train — to stores in Calgary, Edmonton, and Regina.

The Canadian Pacific Railway completed Canada's first coast-to-coast route in 1885. Before the Great War, it was Canada's only transcontinental railway, dominating travel in the west. The Grand Trunk Railway and Canadian Northern Railway dominated train travel in the east. By 1923, the federal government had bought and amalgamated both these lines, creating Canadian National Railways, or CNR.

The companies competed for Christmas contracts from Eaton's

and Simpson's, and department stores whose mail-order departments shipped tons of stock. CPR and CNR shipped millions of Christmas trees every yule. Passengers were the biggest cash cow for railways. Easterners went west to see family. Westerners went east to Toronto, Montreal, Halifax. Some boarded ships for the old country. Old countries. CPR owned ocean liners.

CNR called itself "The National Way." "Let us help plan your Christmas Trip whether Eastbound or Westbound." That particular CNR ad featured an illustration of a grandmother — bespectacled, hair in a bun. The tag line: "They're fixing things for Christmas in Your Old Home Town." Railways cajoled customers at Christmas, trading on homesickness and guilt. "Some rather narrow-minded people think that there's a little too much overeating in Dickens and so on," said a CPR ad:

H'm. Times have changed. But the only thing Dickens hated was the solitary man. He hated him all the time, but most of all the kind of man who couldn't mix sociably and helpfully with his fellow creatures at this one season of the year that is a festival of human fellowship. Dickens wouldn't have had much use for the man who laughs at the idea of going back home for Christmas.

Snowstorms. Technical troubles. Travellers leaving late. It happened every holiday: some Canadians spent their Christmases aboard trains.

The CPR commissioned special Christmas menus for their dining cars. Rous and Mann printed them; the Group of Seven's A. J. Casson illustrated many of them. In 1930, he painted an eighteenth-century Christmas scene. A family in powdered periwigs decorating a tree — anachronistic in the extreme.

Rail lines had radio towers erected along their routes. Come Christmas, the towers beamed out broadcasts of Santa, speaking, singing. Onboard, public-address systems played Christmas music. Passengers could send telegram greetings — Santagrams — to relatives waiting up ahead. On Christmas Eve, porters placed stockings outside the bunks of sleeping tots. On a train departing Moncton on Christmas Eve in 1883, they decorated a tree with "oranges, apples and empty liquor bottles."

"A burly, gruff, reserved but kindly man," is how Margaret Betts described her grandfather in *Trains* magazine. Betts's grandfather was a CPR engineer working out of Halifax during the Depression.

Her grandfather's route took him westward. In winter, he often ordered his firetender to shovel coal off of the coal car and onto the tracks. Children collected the coal. It heated the homes of the poor.

"Every year, just at Christmastime, he would extravagantly buy several large bags of oranges." Betts's grandfather could not eat oranges — he was allergic to them. He tossed them off the train, too. As his train passed, children discovered "oranges all along the tracks, gleaming brightly amidst the black lumps of coal."

CPR porters permitted special behaviour at Christmastime. Spontaneous singalongs among passengers. In 1911, a Toronto theatre troupe took a train to Montreal, to perform *The Chocolate Soldier*, an operetta composed by Oscar Straus. Companies mounted it at Christmastime in the days before productions of Tchaikovsky's *The Nutcracker* became ubiquitous.

It was Christmas Eve. The company's carpenter put up a tree in the passenger car. A Miss Pelham played Santa Claus. Santa led the singing and gift-giving and revelry. "The whole company . . . became children again for a couple of hours."

"The guests at a large hotel in a large city on Christmas day are divided into two classes," said the Montreal *Gazette* in 1904. "They either have no homes, or else no possible means of getting to such as they have." A Christmas tradition involved newspapers printing pieces about the "blue, down-in-the-mouth crowd, Christmas hotel guests," who, the paper said, passed the day swapping stories about Christmases gone by.

Stranded salesmen turned their attentions to staff — girls who manned telephone switchboards. A single girl, the paper said, received sixty boxes of candy.

The Château Frontenac in Quebec. The Banff Springs Hotel. The Royal York in Toronto. All were built by Canadian Pacific in the first decades of the century. The CNR ran the Château Laurier, among others.

Railways decorated their grand hotels in grand style. Evergreen festoons wrapped around and between pillars, silver stars suspended from balconies. Holly ran rampant. Christmas trees held court in rotundas. The Empress Hotel erected a "monster," "the largest ever seen in Victoria."

Hotels adorned restaurants with game. At the King Edward in Toronto, sides of pork and beef dangled over street-front entrances. Chefs went to town. According to one ad, the chef at the Empress Hotel in Victoria was "a master in the preparation of Christmas viands," such as antelope.

Holidays at hotels became *au courant*, thanks to Canada's railways. More Canadians travelled, and Canada had more hotels to travel to. Canadians spent Christmas at hotels in their hometowns. For fun.

"Spirit of Christmas Is Found in Hotels," read a headline in a Prairie newspaper. Hotel restaurants planned holiday menus and Christmas parties for kiddies. Porters suited up as Santa. The Ritz-Carlton in Montreal staged a fancy-dress ball. All ladies went home with hand-painted banners.

A decade after describing the "down-in-the-mouth" scenes of Christmas day, the *Gazette* revisited Montreal's main hotels. "Everywhere the bright colors are hung, and the mottoes bid everybody be happy." Hotels were transforming themselves. Hoteliers gladdened lobbies with imported holly and mistletoe, fir boughs from Laurentian farms. "One noticeable development, however, is the demand for the bright red contrast to the green, which is provided by the now popular poinsettia plant."

The Empress was a CPR hotel. For Christmas 1928, it staged an "Olde English" Christmas. Hundreds of Victorians seated in the ballroom. A jester pranced in, in jester's cap. Jingling bells. Stewards costumed in Elizabethan stomachers and stiff ruffs dragged a yule log. Silver trumpets blared, and minstrels announced the chef, who bore a boar's head covered in words and figures made of butter. "Best Wishes" piped across the snout; deer piped onto the neck. But wild boars were scarce in British Columbia. Instead, the Empress served the head of a domestic pig, with tusks tacked on.

In 1929, CPR advertised the Empress as a Christmas destination. It expanded its Yuletide Festival. Actors performed scenes from Dickens, the script prepared for the company by the Dickens Society of Canada. The festival's musical director prepared a new arrangement of *Christmas with Herrick*, a ballad opera in which wassailers wassailed, and dancers danced Devonshire dances.

On Christmas Eve, the hotel presented a Nativity play written by Alexander Ramsay — a Victorian, a captain in the Canadian military — enacted entirely by "Indians." According to an advertising booklet published by the Empress: "Among the Indians there is no tale in the Bible story which has appealed more to the imagination than that of the Nativity."

Needless to say, the Empress doesn't do this anymore.

In 1939, the Toronto chapter of the National Model Railroad Association built Jasper National Park, in miniature, in a room over Union Station. Five hundred and seventy-five feet of track. Mountains of plaster of Paris and asbestos wool on wooden frames.

Waterfalls. Woods. The chapter did it all, cars included. The locomotive took a year and a half to complete. Chapter members considered store-bought models to be toys. "The main thing for the layman to remember," wrote *Maclean's*, "is that the model railway builders take their hobby seriously. The term 'toy' is a fighting word. The actual model railway fraternity is for men only; women and children needn't apply."

Most men didn't have time to construct complicated layouts. The Lionel Corporation did it for them. Locomotives, passenger cars, freight cars. A milk car with a mechanical milkman who unloaded cans. A mail car that collected mail bags on the fly.

Montreal's Trainatorium operated on Sherbrooke Street in the 1950s, specializing in Lionel goods. Customers could find switches, stations, bridges, signals, gates. Smoke pellets spewed smoke from the funnels of electric engines. An oil derrick gushed something resembling oil. "Lionel equipment is designed to look as much like the real thing as possible." Kids were permitted to operate the trains. For fifteen minutes. They paid a quarter for the privilege.

Toy trains had become "model railroads." Hobbies, not toys. As toy train historian Pierce Carlson wrote, "The cheerful, brightly coloured, imaginative, and rugged toy train has been transformed into the technically perfect, cold and delicate, scale model."

Louis Marx still sold toy train sets. But kids became less and less interested. The age of train travel was ending. Kids wanted toy automobiles, airplanes. Battery-operated, radio-controlled. "According to some toy buyers," said *Maclean's* in 1958, "there has been a fall-off in model railroading due to the competition of television."

Louis Marx's company went under in the 1970s. "Now all the train buyers are adults," wrote Carlson. "Children are no longer interested in finding trains under the Christmas tree."

18

WRAPPING PAPER

"WHAT MAKES A well-wrapped gift?" asks Sharon Younger. "Never leave tape showing. Paper must be tight to the box. Can't be loose or puffy. Seams in the back should be centred. Crease the edges after you finish wrapping. Sharp corners at the ends. That's where people have the most difficulty."

Younger's been in the gift-wrapping business since the 1970s. "I did wrapping at The Bay. I did wrapping at Holt Renfrew. I've been doing it for three years for Hazelton Lanes." Hazelton Lanes is a shopping mall in downtown Toronto. "It's a very stylish, up-to-the-moment, distinctive, fashion-oriented mall. So they want the wrapping to reflect the gift."

Younger is chief wrapper. Her headquarters: a room tucked behind Guest Services. Two banquet tables, gift boxes, a small staff. "I hire people in the season. People that I know can wrap. I have a network of friends I've worked with at a booth in previous years. And I do meet people and you see, 'Oh, they're a good wrapper.'

"Still," Younger says, she "can show anybody how to wrap a gift properly in ten minutes."

How, I wonder, does a person become a gift-wrapping pro?

"I was raised in Thunder Bay," Younger says. "I would go out and buy my gift wrapping at the drugstore. Or at Chapple's department store. I had a cardboard box wrapping station where I would keep all the rolls and bows. And keep it from year to year. I had as much wrapping paper as I did Christmas decorations for the tree.

"My father didn't wrap. He would sit with a glass of Christmas cheer and watch *A Christmas Carol* while the rest of the family wrapped our gifts — and his. My sisters and my brothers, we were all a little artistic, and we'd try to outdo one another with wrapping and ribbons and bows."

I visit Younger on a slow day in December. She's wrapping a pair of suspenders. "At Hazelton Lanes," she says, "they sell beautiful beaded dresses. They cost thousands of dollars. I have to be very careful; a beaded dress can't have any kinds of creases or flat folds. With expensive items — dresses, silk blouses — there's a special way that I have to tissue them in order not to harm the garment. There are two 'oohs' in wrapping. The first is when someone sees the beautiful wrapped gift under the tree. The second is when they open up the gift and see the tissuing."

Surprise could be considered the third ooh. "I do get guys who say, 'I don't want to put this little jewellery box under the tree because then she'll know what it is.' So we put it in a box, put it in another box, put it in another box. Or we'll make a Christmas cracker. Use a roll of wrapping paper — the cardboard roll inside. I have had a few challenges over the years. A pair of snowshoes. Where do you find a box to fit that? You don't. So the people I was wrapping with at the time, we cut cardboard to fit all around it and made it into the shape of a whale. And then we wrapped the whale."

Furs, silk, diamonds — Younger handles the world's most handsome goods. And makes them handsomer.

"It's a privilege," Younger says. "I get to see everybody's Christmas gifts. I'm like Santa."

Santa Claus didn't wrap gifts. Not in the nineteenth century. He hung toys on Christmas trees. On Christmas Eve. I have an old photo. It shows a tree in a Prairie home. Dolls hang from it, like things the Red River washed ashore.

In the late 1800s, Montreal's Teutonia Glee Club held an annual Christmas festival at their club rooms on St. Catherine Street. "Members wishing to present one another with Christmas souvenirs are requested to deliver such in the club rooms," the club instructed in 1885, "well wrapped up and with the name of the party they are intended for on the wrapper."

With what did Teutonians wrap? Parcel paper. Or writing paper. Wrapping paper hadn't been invented.

Parcel paper. "We keep in store all weights and sizes of Brown, Manilla & White Wrappings," advertised a stationer in Halifax in 1899. Druggists wrapped drugs in it. Launderers, laundry. Buy a bauble at Birks? It came wrapped in brown. By Confederation, mills in Quebec were making most of the country's supply.

Then there was stationery. Papeteries, for writing. It was common, inexpensive. "All the presents are done up in white paper and tied with silver cord," an Atlantic newspaper said. White paper made even the smallest gift surprising. And snowy.

Then there were fancy papers. Tissue was fancy, used by jewellers, confectioners. White tissue paper was part of their work. They imported it from Britain.

It wasn't cheap. In 1868, a Montreal stationer advertised tissue paper, alongside gilt, silvered, and glazed papers. Papers for the rich, to send to the rich. Or to scrapbook. Scrapbooks were a novelty.

Canadians treasured tissue. Canadian women, that is. They'd save it up to use at Christmastime. "The last packages may need to have the rose-coloured papers wrapped about them and the dainty ribbons tied," wrote a writer in *The Halifax Herald*, "for a Christmas gift loses half its sweetness unless it is prettily put up. . . ."

Tissue became more common. Prices plummeted, cheaper grades showed up. The Dennison Manufacturing Company of Massachusetts made tissue in scores of colours. Crepe paper was Dennison's cash cow. Or, as one Halifax newspaper called it, "crinkly tissue for decorating."

"The most decorative of all materials," boasted Dennison. It marketed crepe paper as a craft supply. Booklets taught customers how to make crepe-paper costumes, crepe-paper hats. How to weave crepe-paper baskets. Dennison's Christmas line included printed crepe. A Santa Claus print, a team of reindeer flying a sleigh across the sky. Printed crepe could be pinned to walls. Crepe is stretchy, hard to tear. It made fine gift wrap

Dennison also invented the gift tag. To be tied or glued to presents. "When the Dennison Manufacturing Co., at their retail store in Boston, in December, 1901, showed a shipping tag printed with a simple spray of holly and berries, they little thought it was the wedge which would open a large and profitable trade to stationers all over the world."

Dennison got its start in boxes. Paper boxes. Workers glued them by hand at home. Jewellers, stationers, confectioners — certain industries used boxes by the boatload. To expedite box-making, Dennison developed die-cut equipment. It developed holly boxes, paper boxes printed with a holly pattern. Jewellers, stationers, and confectioners used them at Christmas.

"To have all Yuletide 'Gift' parcels given special attention is undoubtedly a boost for the merchant. How can this additional service be rendered without incurring heavy expense?" asked a Canadian trade paper.

Copp Clark in Toronto copied Dennison. It made holly boxes for the Canadian market. Boxes for brooches, shirts, ties, scarves, socks, suspenders. Six sizes in all. Copp Clark marketed them to the trade. Shops put stock in holly boxes, to make them seem gifty. By 1908, Copp Clark also offered holly paper — parcel paper printed with a pattern. Dennison had developed it as an economical alternative to boxes.

Joyce Hall managed a gift shop in Kansas City with his brothers. They printed their own Christmas cards. Their tissue came from Dennison. "Gift-wrapping paper," Hall wrote in his autobiography, "consisted only of plain white, red and green tissue and one holly pattern."

Days before Christmas 1918, Hall had sold out of tissue. He tried something else — stocking a sheaf of fancy papers from France. They were meant to line envelopes. Hall sold them as gift wrap. They sold out. The following holiday, Hall bundled three sheets to a pack. These sold out, too. In 1922, Hall Brothers unveiled a line of wrapping paper. "Gift dressing," it was called. "To all practical purposes, an entire new industry had been born," Joyce Hall wrote.

Reindeer, Santas, poinsettia plants — the earliest wrapping papers boasted all the standard tropes, printed on sulphite paper. Colours bled. Prints blurred. They were cheap. Flint papers had a high gloss, akin to patent leather. They'd been polished in production with a flint stone. Papers came in solid colours, and a slew of stocks. The cheapest: groundwood. The finest: book paper. Dennison sold black paper — "Leatherette," they called it.

The Buzza Company of Minnesota created "Aer-O-Art" wrappings — paper onto which patterns had been airbrushed — no printing, lithographing, or mechanical means involved. Each sheet was "an individual, distinctive, hand-decorated art product."

The first foils came from Switzerland — aluminum foil laminated to paper. The laminate was asphaltum. Sometimes it spotted the foil. Until the Swiss invented a new glue, only deep colours could be done: silver, gold, red, green. After they invented it, Canada got pastel foils. And print foils.

Canada Metal Company established a separate division to manufacture foil paper. Canada Foils Ltd. of Toronto offered foil paper, foil ornaments, and foil torn into strips, also known as icicles.

"Foils were really big in the 1980s," Sharon Younger says. "Customers still like them. At Hazelton Lanes, we have a silver shiny paper and a gold." Younger has never seen black gift wrap. She'd buy it if she did. With brown accents, she says, it would be perfect for gentlemen.

"Red and green are always popular," she says. "That's never going to go away. And we have a classic print with Christmas trees. I do think that's more *de rigueur* right now. Muted prints. At Hazelton Lanes, it's a very discerning clientele. Some will even go so far as to say, 'I want this ribbon with that.'"

During the Great Depression, Canadians couldn't buy big gifts. So they bought gift wrapping. Wrapping paper was now plentiful. Eaton's stocked products from Norcross, an American firm based in New York. "Gift wrappers" is what they called their line: papers printed with Christmas snowflakes and stars. Scottie dogs.

At Merritton, Ontario, Interlake Tissue Mills opened a mill to manufacture tissue and crepe — "Excellent for all Decorative Purposes." In Montreal, Perkins Tissue Mills produced "A Decorative Paper for Every Decorative Purpose."

In 1930, Dennison opened a 29,000-square-foot factory in Drummondville, Quebec. Where "Dennison goods were made by Canadian labour for Canadian use." The factory employed hundreds of workers. Dennison solicited "sketches from the best gift wrap artists in Canada and the United States and selected the finest of their designs." Gift-wrap artists painted or sketched designs onto illustration board. Calligraphers added lettering by hand, usually in India ink. Plate-makers etched the designs onto copperplated rotogravure cylinders. Intaglio, the process was called. It's still called that. A cylinder could press hundreds of thousands of reproductions onto paper.

Canadians snapped up gift wrapping. The problem was, Canadians didn't know how to wrap gifts. At Robert Simpson's Yonge Street store, clerks displayed empty boxes wrapped in Christmas paper, "so that customers may see just how artistically a gift may be 'fixed up.'"

A truck travelled the country — Perkins Tissue Mills paid for it — equipped with a calliope and a loudspeaker "through which victrola records may be played." The truck stopped at fairs and festivals. Display windows in the back showcased gifts wrapped in Perkins products.

Coutts-Hallmark issued instructions in *The Art of Gift Wrapping*, a booklet for sale at stationers'. "Beautifully wrapped gifts are easily created," it says, "but they can't just happen." Dennison offered advice in their own pamphlet, *Secrets of Wrapping Glamorous Gift Packages*. Secret one: use fluff. "Fluff" meant doodads. "Make Santa's beard with a bit of pasted-on cotton."

"It is profitable to offer to wrap all merchandise sold in holly-covered paper, or gold or silver paper, with gayly-coloured tape, for a small extra customer." So said a toy trade paper in the 1920s. Retailers realized early on that pretty packing helped sales. And acted as advertising. "To have all Yuletide 'Gift' parcels given special attention is undoubtedly a boost for the merchant."

In 1925, Eaton's introduced a gift-wrapping service. The Christmas Box, it was called, stocked with Norcross paper. The Christmas Box resembled a giant Christmas box. Wrappers waited inside. Wrappers were always women.

In the retail industry, gift-wrapping services became known as "Packaging Bars." "Clerks who have been taught many intricate ways of gift wrapping are the 'barmaids,'" explained a trade journal. In the 1940s, Simpson's in Toronto built a gift-wrap booth on the store's second floor. At Christmastime, the booth employed upwards of twenty-two women.

Holt Renfrew stores wrapped all their gift packages in blue and silver paper. "The most distinctive in the Dominion," said their ads. Hudson Bay stores went one better, offering courses in gift wrapping. "Instructions in making your Christmas gifts look as attractive on the outside as your gift is inside." The course took two days. "Learn how to make those fascinating gift wrappings you've admired!"

Sharon Younger swears this did not happen at Hazelton Lanes. "A fellow came with three identical boxes and three different sets of lingerie. And he said, 'This one is for my wife, this one is for my mistress, and this one is for my girlfriend, and for God's sake, don't mix them up.' I invented the way of keeping gifts straight. It sounds really simple now that everybody does it. Yellow Post-it notes. Once it's wrapped we put the yellow sticky back on the top of the package. My nightmare is to mix up a gift and some woman opens her present on Christmas Day and finds a shaving kit."

Younger has never had to face her nightmare scenario. She's too good. Her concerns are more quotidian. "Paper cuts. I can't say I get too many of those. The problem with hot glue is inevitably you burn your fingers. You don't want hot glue on somebody's angora sweater. I double-loop the tape, or use a glue stick. Gift wrapping is a labour-intensive business. And it's hard on your back. You're bending over that table and sometimes you're lifting extremely heavy gifts, microwaves and such. I can't wait till I can sleep on Christmas Day."

She doesn't sleep, however, until she's wrapped her own gifts. "A colleague of mine does very good wrapping, but when she wraps her own, she sticks everything in a bag. She does so much wrapping during the Christmas season that they stick their own stuff in bags. I'm the opposite. However hard I work on wrapping at work, I feel I have to work harder on the gifts I give away.

"For all that, for all of the work I do making a gift nice, I have a motto: A gift is to be ogled under the tree. It looks nice, it's part of the

Christmas decorations. Once Christmas comes, I do not expect anyone to save the bows or to save the paper or to save the beautiful design. Rip. Tear. It's over. Next year is another year."

19

BOWS

"THIS BOW OF velvet ribbon consists of four or more loops, varying from three to five inches in length. These are wired with small silk-covered wire, tacked to the back of the loops. Allow 8½ inches of ribbon for each loop, but in making up the loops, vary the length; that is, allow 8 inches or a trifle less for some and a trifle more for others."

Spider bows. Diamond bows. Coquette bows. Crescent bows. Buckle bows. Fancy Alsatian bows. Foliage bows. Star bows. Beetle bows. Ear of Corn bows. Meteor bows. Drooping Loop bows. At the turn of the last century, women bought bows. Department stores stocked them in dressmaking and millinery departments. Women without the means to buy bows made them by hand. Instructions for a poinsettia bow appear above.

Bows decorated dresses and wraps, adorned brassieres. Mostly, bows bedecked hats. Dress hats for night, semi-dress hats for day. "In accessories to the costume," said a millinery magazine, "by way of adding a necessary colour note and hint of frivolity, ribbon and bows fill a most important need."

Taffeta, velvet, silk. Ribbons were cloth. Woven, selvaged on the sides. Milliners imported them from mills in Switzerland and France. Dresden ribbon came from Germany. Canadian women knew their weaves. In organdy ribbon, the weave is open. In taffeta ribbon, the weave is tight. Ribbons had numbers — number 5 ribbon was one inch wide, number 9 ribbon was 1½ inches wide. There were dozens of different numbers.

Canadian ladies studied books about making bows. "One of the first essentials to success is the ability to handle ribbons daintily, without creasing or mussing them," read one bow-making booklet. "A clear conception of the bow in mind makes the way easier for the maker."

Bows followed fashion. Aster bows were the rage for a season, supplanted the next season by Aeroplane bows. "New ideas in bows are to be observed, studied and applied," said a bow-making book. "A gift for making graceful bows, like other talents, must be cultivated."

At Christmas, department stores stocked extra ribbon. Periodicals published plans for transforming ribbon into holiday crafts. Ribbon craft, it was called — fancy-work. "[Ribbons] make such charming hairbows for gifts." And sewing aprons, and sachets, and hankie cases. Wrap heavy shirred duchess ribbon around a clothes hanger and *voila!* — fancy padded hangers.

Pincushions were also popular. Shaped like fish, birds, fruit. Too pretty to prick. A pincushion shaped like a lady? Here's how to make it: sew a dress of duchess ribbon, trimmed with baby ribbon; stick a doll in it; stuff the dress with sawdust. My favourite: a ribbon dispenser made of ribbon. "Procure a medium large doll's head with curly hair, fastening it to a little satin bag slashed in the centre front to hold the ribbon doll. The end of the ribbon is drawn through the doll's mouth, and will always be found to run freely."

"There is no ribbon scrap," suggested an old craft manual, "no bit of silk or velvet so inconsequential that it cannot be put to excellent use, making charming Xmas gifts."

Ribbon didn't just make gifts. It made gift wrap.

At Confederation, Canadian merchants tied up packages with twine or cord. Brown cord. Coloured cord appeared in the late 1800s in red and green. Vendors stocked it come Christmastime.

"This is the finest tinsel made and makes a beautiful decoration," boasted an Eaton's ad in *The Halifax Herald* of 1905. Eaton's imported tinsel from Germany: copper wire coated with silver or gold. They sold it by the yard. Canadians cut it up to decorate trees. "All the presents are done up in white paper and tied with silver cord," said the *Herald*, describing a stylish Canadian Christmas scenario. Silver cord, tinsel cord, fancy cord. It had many names. Tinsel twined with cording. It was the first tie intended solely for tying up gifts.

But tinsel cord tarnished. Cloth ribbon, Canadian ladies discovered, was tarnishproof, and more colourful than tinsel cord. Not to mention softer: tinsel cord could cut hands.

Department stores noticed. "Everything here from the narrow Yuletide and Holly ribbons for tying up gifts to wider fancy ribbons for fancy work," said an Eaton's ad of 1910. Ribbon had become *de rigueur*. "Parcels are twice as festive looking when they're all tied up with ribbons," read one Eaton's ad. "Daintily tied up, they are far more acceptable," said the Hudson's Bay Company.

"Yuletide" ribbon was really green or red baby ribbon repackaged as gift wrap. Soon into the new century, they'd started selling cloth ribbon printed with a holly pattern. At the end of the Great War, Canadians could also find mistletoe patterned ribbon. And greeting ribbons — red ribbon with green edging, green ribbon with red edging. Also available were "satin ribbons for tying holly and evergreen wreaths."

The catch: cloth ribbon made bad gift wrap. Bows drooped. Unless the ribbon was starched or stitched. Ribbon stretched. Slipped from gifts. During the early days of the Depression, an American company named Norcross came up with "Tishu-Ties," paper ribbons that were "easy to tie — hard to tear." In Canada, Dennison manufactured Excello ribbon, from cellophane. Norcross came back with cellophane ribbon threaded with cloth threads. Competitors came out with rayon ribbon. Trade names of the time included Glamortie, Facile. Novelty ribbons were printed with Santas, stars, etc. Hallmark's ribbon was of acetate rayon. Stiff, its edges not woven, but fused hard by heat. The cheapest choice was ribbonzene, rayon fibres that were glued together and crimped. Drag it over a scissors' edge and it curls. It's still sold today. It's still the cheapest of ribbons.

Stainproof, rainproof, plastic ribbons stayed in shape. Women taught themselves to loop gift bows. "If bows of ribbon are to be part of the package decoration," said a consultant to department-store gift-wrap bars, "have them made in advance and fastened together with fine wire." Wrappers perfected complicated confections — glamour bows, loops, pinwheels, wreaths, Greeks, hairs, pussycats, figure-eights. Poinsettia bows. Looked sort of like poinsettias.

"I can make bows by hand," says Sharon Younger, chief wrapper at Hazelton Lanes in Toronto. "I do it when I have the time. Talk about the other mark of a professionally wrapped gift — having a bow that's to scale with the package. So many times when you buy a package of bows, if you have a great big coat box, the bow is going to look dwarfed on the box. So I will have to tie the package with a lot of extra ribbon so that I have enough left over to make the big-looped bows so that it matches the scale of the box."

"If you object to tying bows," said *Chatelaine* in 1940, "or find your fingers all thumbs when this part of the business confronts you, just omit them." J. J. Thayer earned a university degree in engineering. In 1951, he invented a machine that made gift wrap bows. He invented different bow-making machines to make different sizes with loops of varying length. A Thayer machine twisted ribbons into roses. He founded Indiana Ribbon in Indiana, his home state.

Thayer's machines automatically applied adhesive patches to bows. Card companies like Hallmark and Carlton developed similar machines. They sold bows by the bag, like spuds. Bows are still sold that way. Almost all are stars — star shapes held together by staples.

20

CHRISTMAS CORSAGES

"LAURELS TO THE members of the second floor Gift Wrap booth," wrote Simpson's *Staff News* in January of 1947. "With 22 girls on the staff . . . thousands of gifts were wrapped during the two weeks immediately preceding Christmas."

The "girls" were women who worked at Toronto's Queen Street store. "About 90 percent of the customers are men," said the *Staff News*. A photograph proved it. A mass of men. A counter that kept them from crushing those who were wrapping. Women in white smocks.

Smocks and corsages of fake flora: plastic poinsettias and ivy and evergreens. Pine needles made of pipe cleaner. Christmas corsages, they were called, worn, in the words of a newspaper ad, by "everyone from debutantes to dowagers." They became fashionable in the 1940s, unfashionable by the 1970s. But they're still around — in attics, on eBay. Doodads decorated them. Plastic bells, glass balls. Styrofoam snowmen that won't melt for a thousand years.

"A Corsage — A gift which shows personality —" according to Campbell's, a Montreal florist. For Christmas 1923, its corsages consisted of "Roses, Violets, Orchids, and other motifs —" Corsages can be worn at the waist or on the wrist. The shoulder's the standard spot. The word *corsage* means "bodice of a dress."

"Corsage flowers are in great demand, particularly to be worn with furs." But the cost was four dollars and up. For four dollars, a family could eat a turkey dinner. "A corsage doesn't just indicate an occasion," said a corsage-making manual, "it also gives an air of importance."

The unimportant and the poor preferred fakes.

Turkeys, geese, ducks — classic Christmas fowl. Canadian women cleaned and cooked them. The feathers they transformed into flowers. Flora from fauna. Feather flowers, the first fakes in Canada. Feathers were cheap, plentiful. Victorian women arranged nosegays in vases or sealed them in shadow boxes.

Or wore them. "Make a spectacular white evening corsage of capon feathers," instructed the manual. "Twenty-five feathers will be needed for a five-flower corsage."

"If one has time and patience to make a number of them," suggested a newspaper article of the 1880s, "paper rosettes are very pretty." Rosettes resemble roses. Roughly. Stamens are circles; petals, squares. Paper flowers wouldn't become more complicated until the 1900s, when cheap crepe papers hit the market. Crepe can be stretched, tinted, cupped, curled, fluted, and fringed without tearing. Interlake Tissue Mills manufactured it at its plant in Merritton, Ontario. The mill published a pamphlet, *The Decorative Use of Crepe Paper*, filled with patterns for paper flowers. Women crafted crepe corsages to give to guests at Christmas parties. A corsage gets crushed? It's a serviette.

"Gala with streamers and replete with fascinating articles for sale," said the Montreal *Gazette* in 1926, "were the eight booths that vied with each other in exhibiting their wares at the Homemakers' Club Christmas bazaar."

At the candy booth, homemade fudge; at the toy booth, homemade dolls. The flower booth had homemade flowers made from ribbon.

Cloth ribbon, velvet, or satin or taffeta. Four yards made a Christmas rose; three, a rosebud. A typical corsage consisted of a rose with a bud surrounded by violets. Women attached them to coat or capelet or *chapeau*.

Rain ruined them. Not to mention moths.

"If there's anything with stronger sales appeal than the current artificial flowers," argued a trade magazine in 1938, "it would be difficult to put a finger on it." The name of the fake flower department at Simpson's Queen Street store was "Flower Lane." It opened in the late 1930s, the first of its kind in Canada. "Those in charge report a lively turnover."

Bouquets bloomed in all the latest molecular arrangements — plastics such as vinyl, polymers such as rayon and, later on, nylon. "For the store, restaurant and hotel décor, their use is wide and varied, as are also the price lines ranging from a few cents to dollars per spray or bloom."

Women adorned Christmas dresses with roses, tulips, violets, orchids. Not Christmas corsages, but corsages that could be worn at Christmas. Like feather flowers, like ribbon roses, like crepe corsages, plastic corsages were utterly un-Christmassy. Gift wrappers changed all that.

At Simpson's Queen Street store, gift wrappers fixed gifts up with bows, big as gift boxes. Glamour bows, loops, pinwheels, wreaths, rosettes. Wrappers fixed them up with fake flowers, velour mistletoe, sprays of sateen holly spray painted silver. Rayon poinsettias in "real" colours.

Wrappers added ornaments to gifts. For oomph. J. G. Fraser Ltd. of Vancouver sold packages of "package ties" — chenille Santas, snowmen, canes, Christmas figures — prefab fluff at pennies a pop. "Tie one on each parcel you wrap." Simpson's carried pine cones painted silver, gold, or red. The supplier? Parks. Pine cones were pure profit for the store.

"It's Christmas Time!" shouted an old Eaton's ad. The Gift Wrap department offered evergreen cones, fake ferns, red plastic berries, and silver bells, all tied up in a shiny bow. An arrangement to attach to gifts. "To pin up as decorations," the ad said. "To wear on your coat."

Fluff had leapt from parcels onto lapels. Christmas corsages — gift dressing for dresses, hybrids of horticulture and holiday decoration. Department stores sold them. Dime stores, too. An Elizabeth Arden perfume package came complete with a tinsel-and-glass Christmas-tree corsage.

In 1955, J. G. Fraser's catalogue of wholesale decorations included corsages. "Silver and lacquered leaves, colourful balls, acorns, mistletoe berries." Gaudy wasn't the word. A certain corsage had "pink satin-embossed leaves with multicolour glitter." At its centre sat a "net poinsettia with gold balls."

Church ladies created corsages to sell at bazaars and fairs. Girl Guides sold them door to door, for fundraising. Ladies' aid societies pinned them to the pillows of hospitalized ladies. *Canadian Home & Hobbycraft* magazine published plans for crafting corsages. "The Christmas season is one of the times when artificial corsages are worn, and milady loves to add a Christmassy dash."

Some women still crave a Christmassy dash. They wear pins. Plastic pins, made in China. Rudolphs with red lights for noses. Rudolph glows for a couple of months, then dies. Santa Clauses with strings between their legs. Tug a string, Santa dances.

Stores sell Christmas roses, gold-plated pins. Tree pins are collectible, costume pieces covered with rhinestones. Tree pins were popular in the 1950s and 1960s, the same time that Christmas corsages were *au courant*. Tree pins are still popular. Vintage pins fetch small fortunes at auction.

Christmas corsages? They're ripe for revival. Some women still make them. Craft-supply stores sell synthetic stamens and stems, but manufacturers abandoned the market years ago. At a recent Gift and Tableware show in Toronto, not a single retailer in sight was selling them.

Fake flowers they did sell. Fakes are perennial sellers, as bouquets, as ornaments. A woman in the market for a Christmas corsage might consider pinning a poinsettia centrepiece to her coat. A holly candle wreath worn on the wrist. To complete the suite: a napkin ring as a ring.

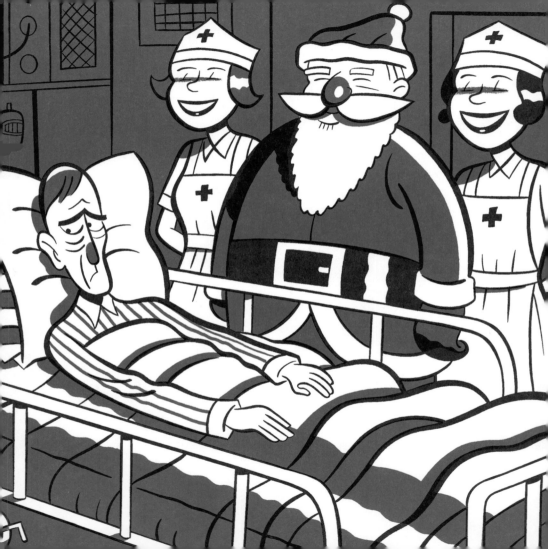

21

CHRISTMAS SEALS

CHRISTMAS EVE, 1895. A tavern on St. Catherine Street in Montreal. Crowded. Clamorous. Arguments arise. There's a scuffle. Gunshots. Medics remove a man to hospital, a bullet lodged in his leg.

Doctors cut into the wound, but can't locate the lead. Weeks later, they X-ray, exposing the patient to radioactive rays for forty-five minutes. The bullet's lodged between tibia and fibula. It's taken out. It's the first X-ray taken in Canada.

Wilhelm Konrad Roentgen discovered X-rays in 1895. Henri Becquerel discovered radioactivity the following year. Hospitals across Canada experimented, converting gas-discharge tubes and static-electricity generators into X-ray apparatus.

CHRISTMAS DAYS

Alexander Graham Bell experimented with radium at his Nova Scotia summer home. He tried to send X-rays down telephone lines. In Montreal, William Osler shoved gallstones into beefsteak and X-rayed them. They didn't show. But other conditions did.

A cough. It comes on as a cough that won't die. Then come fevers. Flaring, fading. This lasts for years. Appetite ebbs, energy ebbs. Chest pains. Coughing brings up blood. The blood's bacterial. *Tubercle bacillus*, the medical name for tuberculosis. TB destroys tissue, creates cavities filled with pus. Respiration becomes impossible. TB also attacks other organs. Bones. Skin. In *A Christmas Carol*, Charles Dickens never specifies Tiny Tim's ailment, but scholars speculate it was probably TB of the spine. TB was tops — Canada's number one killer in Victorian times, in Edwardian times. It acted like a cold or the flu. Sufferers thought themselves healthy, until it was too late. Symptoms took years to appear. "Consumption," Canadians called it. Other aliases included Wasting, the White Plague, Captain of the Men of Death.

A shadow. That's what TB looks like in X-rays, a shadow on the apex of the lung. The shadow is a cavity, or the start of a cavity. With X-rays, TB could be spotted early and treated, by sending the sufferer

254

to a sanatorium. Bed rest. Balanced meals. Fresh air. Sanatoria were out in the country, far from factories.

The problem was that X-rays were expensive. And fragile, exposed as they were on glass plates a foot wide and a foot and a half tall. As for sanatoria, there were none. Not in Canada. Some Canadians sailed to Europe for treatment. The wealthy ones. Poor patients suffered at home, died in hospital.

Anti-TB leagues popped up across the country. Noted doctors founded the Tuberculosis Association of Canada. The association purchased X-ray equipment. It convinced provinces to build sanatoria, and to pay the way for tubercular Canadians who could not afford treatment on their own.

It fundraised. Nothing succeeded like Christmas seals.

In Confederation-era Canada, Christmas presents were presented wrapped in plain white paper. Gift wrap hadn't been invented, nor had Scotch tape. Glue held most packages together; sometimes straight pins, sometimes daubs of sealing wax. Seals appeared — gummed seals — around 1900. Holly sprays were the standard shape. Terriers were popular, patterned after President Theodore Roosevelt's pet dog, Jack.

A decade later, Copp Clark offered the "Canada First" line. "The only line," the company said, "designed entirely by Canadian artists and manufactured by Canadian workmen." Christmas seals shaped like maple leaves, like the Canadian coat of arms. The coat of arms appeared on money, and on the Canadian Red Ensign, which was our flag — until we adopted the Canadian flag, with its maple-leaf design. Its candy-cane colours.

Denmark gave us charity seals. Postmen there sold them. Danes stuck them on cards and gifts. The Danish queen's face graced the seals. The money built sanatoria for sick kids.

In 1907, charity seals came to America. A Delaware sanatorium ran out of funds and was about to shut down, forcing hundreds of patients — infectious patients — into the streets. A Red Cross worker stepped in. Inspired by the Danes, she designed a seal: a holly wreath with bright red berries. She ran off sheets. A newspaper sold them. The sanatorium survived. Thrived.

The Christmas seal campaign spread to Canada. In 1908, Torontonians sold seals, raising capital to build sanatoria in the city and in the Muskoka Lakes region. Saint John joined in: New Brunswick churches sold seals to help Toronto build its sanatoria. Winnipeggers sold more than seals. "The ladies' auxiliary to the Anti-Tuberculosis society will make another effort to-day to dispose of its Christmas stamps, tags and labels," the *Manitoba Free Press* reported. Their earnings were earmarked for Manitoban treatments.

"Wearing the white uniform of a trained nurse and the double red cross badge, symbol of the Anti-Tuberculosis Crusade, these unselfish workers for the relief of the most helpless class in the community, destitute consumptives, will offer the Christmas Seals in packages of ten and twenty-five," announced the Montreal *Gazette*. The nurses stood in department stores. Seals cost a penny apiece. A local artist designed them — red-and-green holly on a white ground.

Saskatchewan sold something else: name tags that looked like gold medals. Give money, get a name tag. Nobody gave money. Some gave promissory notes, then broke their promises. In the 1910s, the Anti-Tuberculosis League scarcely covered their fundraising costs.

Saskatchewan was undaunted. The province conducted Canada's first TB survey, screening a thousand school children. More than half tested positive for the infection. The province offered free treatment to all tuberculosis patients, the first province to do so. Taxpayers coughed up the cash.

The province erected sanatoria in Saskatoon and Fort Qu'Appelle. Christmas was a gay time. Patients ate turkey with all the trimmings. Santa visited tubercular children. Was his beard sewn from surgical masks? In 1928, the province joined a national Christmas seals campaign. The Canadian Tuberculosis Association had centralized Christmas seal sales. An American artist designed the image — reindeer pulling Santa's sleigh. The Canadian Bank Note Company printed the seals. The association distributed them to every city in the country.

Thirty million seals. All sold. Saskatchewan shared the rewards, and built another sanatorium in Prince Albert. They set about X-raying the province's entire population. "The Saskatchewan Anti-Tuberculosis League," said a TB society newsletter, "has created for itself a most remarkable field of activity and an equipment and programme unequalled anywhere, unless it might be in Denmark."

"About forty countries carry on the fight against tuberculosis by means of Christmas Seals," reported an ad for Christmas seals. It appeared in a Christmas number of *The Sanitarium Sun*, a newsletter written and edited by patients at the Muskoka Sanitarium near Gravenhurst. "What a gay time is Christmas for us here in the San," said an editorial in the Christmas 1932 *Sun*. "No need for home folks to worry over us or to be sorry that we must spend it in a hospital." Another year, the San restated the same message satirically. "To those of you who are unfortunate enough to be able to go home for a few days, we can wish you a pleasant journey and a most enjoyable holiday with your wives, children, sweethearts, mothers-in-law, fathers-in-law and other dubious characters."

"This must be my fourth Christmas in the San," wrote an anonymous columnist in the 1938 number. "Kelly wanted company — poor guy, so darn lonesome for his wife and kids . . . Christmas Eve does that to one . . . Golly, that old moon is riding high tonight . . . Be nice skating on the lake . . . Poor Kelly, I bet he's looking out his window, too . . . Down at the Christmas tree I thought he was going to bust out crying . . . That surely was some tree — lights, tinsel, packages, gifts for everyone. . . ."

In 1934, *The Sanitarium Sun* printed letters from bedridden patients:

Dear Santa Claus: Please bring us the "gift of patience" so that we will rest and regain our health. Harry MacKinnon.

Dear Santa: Just a line from an old boy of yours. The one thing I would like best would be a photo of Greta Garbo. Yours in dissipation, James Charlton.

Hello Santa: Do you think you could bring me the photos of all the Maple Leaf Hockey stars, also a hockey stick? Thanking you, I remain your little lover of sports, Mable Bogg.

Nurses decorated the tree. Nurses sang carols, wrapped gifts. "Each Christmas every patient of Muskoka Hospital receives a gift from Santa Claus, all nicely wrapped in Christmassy paper." The sanitarium paid for presents with funds from private donors and donations from chapters of both the IODE and the Eastern Star. "The National Sanitarium Association always steps into the breach if there is any threatened shortage which might result in some patient being overlooked when Santa visits the hospital."

At Christmas, sleighfuls of letters and gifts arrived from faraway families. Patients didn't have much opportunity to shop. Available in the main building were *Christmas for Everyone* and *The House of Christmas*, booklets written by Rev. Grover Livingstone, a local clergyman. They made "suitable gifts to be sent from the San." *The Sanitarium Sun* promoted another gift idea: a subscription to *The Sanitarium Sun*.

"Come aboard and have your X-ray taken." A voice big as Santa's, booming across a harbour. Washing in across the water from somewhere out at sea.

"We are here now to carry out a tuberculosis survey of every man, woman and child in your community. There's no need to dress up. And you don't have to undress for your X-ray."

A white ship appeared. With a red cross on a white flag. The double-barred cross, symbol of TB. The ship: the M.V. *Christmas Seal*. She travelled around Newfoundland and back — 6,000 miles of coast — anchoring at hundreds of coastal communities unreachable by roads.

"Please come on board for your free chest X-ray. This is a service made possible by your Christmas seal dollars. Now remember, TB can be passed from the sick to the well. And no homes are safe, my friends, until all homes are safe."

In 1950, about 5 percent of Newfoundland's population, 20,000 people, had active pulmonary tuberculosis. Newfoundland had one sanatorium, which had a waiting list of 2,000 names. The San had 200-odd beds.

The Newfoundland Tuberculosis Association bought a ship — war surplus sold off by the United States Air Force. In World War II, she'd served as rescue vessel. In 1949, the association recommissioned her with monies raised from Christmas seal sales. A floating X-ray clinic, the first of its kind in the world. Crew included radiography technicians, a health educator, a doctor, a nurse, and Captain Peter Troake. As Troake steered into bays, he'd blast oompah music, bark over loudspeakers. Part carny, part cheerleader, cajoling people to come. I've reproduced some of his words above.

According to a CBC reporter, the Captain was "a Pied Piper, luring young and old to the boat for an X-ray." Towns turned out en masse to meet the *Christmas Seal*. "Newfoundland hospitality is never lacking no matter what the occasion and while the visit's seriousness is never forgotten," said *The Atlantic Advocate*, "there is a holiday air of excitement." These holiday celebrations consisted of tests, vaccinations, and injections.

Margaret Mercer worked as a nurse aboard the *Christmas Seal* for eleven years. "It was really a big day when she would arrive with her flag flying and her loudspeaker going and her music," she told CBC Radio. "Then we would be assigned to do a part of the coast, and maybe that would include 5,000 X-rays.

"When the person would come in to be registered," she said, "they were given a card with a number on it and a name. So on our return trip we wouldn't call anybody's name over the P.A. system, we'd call the numbers. And there they would stand, looking over the numbers, and thanking God, 'They don't want me.'

"But then you would see maybe four, maybe five, maybe six, could be ten, dropping the card and getting in their dory or just coming over the hill if it was in the wharf, to get this message to know what was wrong. They would be told it could be that this was just old scars showing, or it could be that they had pneumonia in the past. Or, sad to say, it could be tuberculosis.

"Now this didn't happen very often, but maybe once or twice in my eleven years. We'd just come in and anchor, put on our music, and the doctor or the X-ray technician would say, 'We are very glad to be able to tell you that we did not find one case of tuberculosis in your community.' Immediately the guns would salute. And we could hear the guns until we were way out of sight."

The M.V. *Christmas Seal* is no longer. The association decommissioned it in 1970. TB had been nearly eradicated. In 1977, the Canadian Tuberculosis Association took a new name: the Canadian Lung Association. The Lung Association doesn't hand-sell Christmas seals anymore; it mails them out. Eight million a year. Canadians remit however much money they please. The association stages a design competition. Hundreds enter. Past winners include painters from P.E.I., Alberta, Ontario. The association prefers tried-and-true Christmas icons — snowmen, reindeer — that reproduce well when shrunken to stamp size.

Money raised is divided among provincial Lung Associations. The goal: to "improve respiratory health," defend it from sundry diseases like asthma, chronic bronchitis, emphysema. And tuberculosis. TB's not gone. The germ's grown resistant to drugs. It attacks the poor, those with depressed immune systems. Still, it's not nearly as common as it once was. The Lung Association aims to keep it this way. Stamp it out. Lick TB. Lick seals.

Unless you're ill. Germs survive for months in dry spit.

22

CHRISTMAS CARDS

WRITE A LETTER. Fold it up. Seal with a splash of wax. This is how Canadians mailed letters before the 1840s. That's when Canadian stores introduced envelopes to their inventories.

Early envelopes were handmade. Stationers pressed tin forms to stacks of paper, then cut the outlines of the forms with shoemakers' knives. They folded the sheets with bone folders or thimbles. Glued them shut with gum.

Personal envelopes could be sealed by licking a "lick of gum" on the sealing fold. Business envelopes were tied shut. Beans, clothes, seeds — business envelopes carried saleables across Canada. Post office inspectors could open them for inspection.

Canadians mailed Christmas cards *sans* envelopes. Envelopes were expensive and unnecessary. Christmas cards then were almost always what we would call postcards.

In the 1880s, a Halifax stationer started attaching a white envelope to each Christmas card he sold — even postcards — to preserve them as they passed through the Canadian postal service.

Stationers everywhere took to the idea. The post office was unprepared. "The senders of Christmas cards should carefully bear in mind that . . . they may not be sent in closed envelopes," cautioned a Canadian newspaper.

It cost a penny to send a card domestically. If the envelope was unsealed. A letter in a sealed envelope cost more — three pennies, prepaid. "This caution is given because it is noticed that already the senders of Christmas cards are falling into the mistake of mailing them in closed envelopes." Cards without proper postage went to the dead letter office, a fate "calculated to provoke feelings antagonistic to the superfine Christian spirit of which these cards are of course an embodiment."

In 1898, Canada's postmaster general proposed a new plan: for the price of a two-cent postage stamp, a card could be delivered to any point in the British Empire, in any envelope.

Queen Victoria approved the plan, and the stamp. Though it didn't bear her portrait; instead, it depicted a map of the world. With the British Empire inked in red. Ink that bled. The Empire seemed to extend into the world's lavender-ink oceans.

Issued on December 25, the stamp read, "Xmas 1898." Canada's first Christmas stamp. The world's first Christmas stamp. It accelerated the acceptance of envelopes and the acceptance of Christmas cards by Canadians. In 1898, Christmas cards weren't all that old.

Sir Henry Cole invented the Christmas card. Another man designed it, lithographed it, and hand-coloured it. But Cole commissioned it, so it's his invention. This was in London in 1846. Cole ordered a thousand cards. Ivy-edged, the centre scene depicted a family feasting at Christmas.

Cole sold the cards in an art shop he owned. Cole's coterie purchased them. His coterie had cash. His coterie included Albert, the Prince Consort, the man who introduced the Christmas tree tradition to Britain.

In 1868, *The Times* of London referred to Christmas cards for the first time. For the first time, cards were mass-produced, thanks to a process called chromolithography: a picture is painted onto tinplate, then pressed onto paper. Red ink's brushed onto the plate. The paper's pressed again. Blue's added next, then yellow. Chromolithography made colouring cheap. Transfer paper made it faster. Ditto power-driven flatbed printing machines.

The English illustrated Christmas cards with holly and ivy, Beefeaters, armoured knights. A writer described one Victorian Christmas card thusly: "Cupids shovelling Christmas pudding into wheelbarrows."

Louis Prang was America's main maker. Prang sold cards shaped like thistles, butterfly wings, saddles, canoes, life preservers. Cards shaped like mince pies, "full of spicy, savory quotations and meaty chunks of wisdom, easy to digest."

Canada's carriage trade bought British cards. And German cards. Young women displayed them in Christmas card albums. By 1879, an anonymous columnist for The Montreal *Gazette* could complain of "the average stereotyped style of cards which are showered on us *ad nauseam* at this festive season." The remedy? Canadian cards.

Canadian stationers lithographed their own lines. Henderson's of Montreal issued a line called "The Snow Balls." On the cards were snowshoers, the ice railway, the Tuque Bleue snowslide, the ice palace of the winter carnival. "The cards," wrote the *Gazette*'s anonymous columnist, "are especially suited for sending to friends across the 'herring pond' or further away."

Some stationers sold Christmas cards that folded over. Fold-overs, they were called, or French folds. They're standard nowadays, but then, they were expensive and rare. Uncommon till the 1920s.

Tom Thomson. Franklin Carmichael. F. H. Varley. Arthur Lismer. Frank Johnston. All associated with the Group of Seven. Before they were big, they designed Christmas cards for Rous and Mann. Rous and Mann also made advertising calendars and books. It printed Jean de Brebeuf's *The First Christmas Carol*, an English translation of "Jesus Ahatonhia," the "Huron Indian Carol."

Christmas cards were the firm's bread and butter. Rous and Mann ran a factory in Toronto where an entire floor was devoted to card production. Artists worked in-house. Winter scenes were common. Christmas card production started in spring. The artwork went unsigned. Which did Tom Thomson or Varley work on? It's hard to know. Rous and Mann folded in the 1970s — all the catalogues, all the sketches, all the time cards destroyed when the factory changed hands.

By the 1920s, the Group of Seven were familiar figures on the Canadian art scene. Rous and Mann introduced the Canadian Artists line of

Christmas cards, featuring former employees, and others. Paul Caron contributed a card "full of genuine Quebec feeling," according to *The Canadian Magazine*. A. J. Casson's cards conjured small-town Ontario. Smothered under snow.

"Here we find examples of the work of Gagnon, Brigden, Jackson, Haines, Turner, Casson, Harris, Banting, Bridgewood, Caron, Johnston, Jefferys, MacDonald, Palmer," said *The Chatelaine*. "There is no other country in which its Christmas cards provide so impressive an exhibit of the work of its leading artists."

Presswork and paper were superlative. Some cards were hand-coloured. The National Gallery exhibited the cards at Christmas every year for years. Liberty's, a London department store, carried them. "There is now a steadily growing demand for them at . . . many of the larger stores in London."

In 1931, A. Y. Jackson wrote a note to artist Anne Savage confessing that he was "pretty well fed up" with Rous and Mann. "Rous and Mann have about fifty artists working for them now and it has become a rather undignified scramble to be in."

It was January. "Coutts the Christmas card people wanted to see me a couple days ago," he wrote. "There is a decided possibility that

American cards are going to be put off the market, and it will mean a much bigger business for Canadian firms."

American cards would indeed disappear from the Canadian market under a trade blockade. Jackson asked Savage to submit a couple of Christmas designs to Coutts. He inked a similar note to Charles Comfort in June. "W. Coutts & Co. are getting out a line of Christmas cards to be known as the 'Painters of Canada' series," he wrote.

Anne Savage submitted a painting. Comfort sent a snowshoer striding across a snowy field. Jackson corralled designs from Frank Carmichael, Lawren Harris, F. H. Brigden, Sarah Robertson, Yvonne McKague — forty of Canada's finest. Dr. Banting submitted a snowy scene. Coutts silkscreened images by hand, one by one, onto greeting-card blanks. Carmichael supervised. Each card came out unique. The cards were wrapped in sheets of oil silk imprinted with a biographical sketch of the artists. Every store in the Dominion stocked them that Christmas.

The cards flopped.

In late 1931, Coutts travelled to Kansas City. He met with Joyce Hall. Hall and his brothers had founded Hall Brothers Stationery, which became Hallmark in 1932. Coutts asked to produced Hallmark designs in Canada. He showed Hall his latest works: the Painters of Canada series. Hall admired the designs, the careful production. He agreed to Coutts's request. No contract, no memos, a handshake deal.

For Coutts, it was a coup. He'd been scouring Canada and the United Kingdom for suitable stationery designs. No longer. Hallmark employed scores of artists. Coutts imported print-ready positives, skipping a costly part of the production process.

Hallmark bought shares in Coutts's company in the 1940s, then bought the company outright. Coutts continued to work well into his eighties. He continued to produce the Painters of Canada line, commissioning images from Manley, from Currin. The flat fee artists received was twenty-five dollars a card.

Coutts never tried silkscreening again. After 1931, cards were lithographed. The silkscreened images are now collector's items, rarely appearing at auction and fetching many hundreds of dollars. Hallmark Canada had a complete collection until the 1980s, when it donated them to the National Gallery in exchange for a tax credit.

"I'm lucky," says Sam Paonessa. "I work surrounded by history." Paonessa is showing me around Hallmark's headquarters in Toronto's north end. It's appointed with paintings.

"Mr. Coutts acquired a lot of the original Christmas-card art for the corporate collection," Paonessa says. For example, Coutts bought a complete set of Nicholas Hornyansky's Toronto prints from the 1930s and 1940s.

"Frank Panabaker was another favourite," says Paonessa. Panabaker specialized in depicting back roads of Southern Ontario. Before Coutts died in 1973, he asked that a Panabaker be included in the Painters of Canada line every year for as long as Panabaker was active.

Paonessa is Hallmark's creative design specialist. "I've been working on cards ever since I started." That was in 1983. Paonessa's in charge of the Painters of Canada line. "We need, depending on the year, seven or eight designs. I'm involved in selecting images from the archives, sourcing out the artists, dealing with the artists one-on-one, or sometimes even with museums, galleries, estates."

Paonessa's at work on the cards a year before they hit stores. His stable of artists includes John Joy. Joy's a Toronto artist, a jolly man with a white beard. He poses as Santa. Paonessa paints him. "I have a good handle on what images do well," he says. "Based on our history and sales history. One thing that never fails is a horse and sleigh. It seems to sell and sell, even in this day and age."

Paonessa shows me a dummy. For a book: *The Art of Greeting Cards: Painters of Canada Series*. His predecessor, Michael Chortsky, compiled it in the 1980s, but it was never published. It contains over

200 cards. More than a third are sleighing scenes. "To boot," Chortsky wrote, "there is an ox-drawn sledge, dog teams, and a toboggan pulled by a labrador." Most of the paintings predate 1940. Coutts was fascinated by teams. A runaway team of horses killed his father when he was a lad.

Paonessa's a painter, the only one employed at Hallmark Canada. "We have graphic artists here, it's all digital. They're doing catalogues, point-of-purchase packaging, whatever is needed for Canadian needs. I'm the main artist in terms of doing creative product marketing design." Paonessa paints new Christmas cards every year.

He paints at work. His studio is a couple of cubicles pushed together on the second floor of the company. From his easel, he can see the employee parking lot. Highway 401. Beyond it, bank towers. On his easel: wintry woods.

"I grew up in an Italian family," says Sam Paonessa. "It was always lots of fun. I always wanted to get more stuff. But I remember lots and lots of snow. When I'm thinking of Christmases past, what it was like when I was a kid, I always think of snow."

He shows me a painting. A creek crusted with ice. Snow on the ice. Snow on the ground. Snow on the trees. The snow's full of pinks, lilacs, greys. "My paintings always have tons of snow. I work hard at it."

He recently completed a painting of Banff, Alberta: Mount Rainer sheathed in snow. It'll appear in a line of Christmas cards for western Canada. "We do regional Christmas cards," he says. "We do Central, which takes care of Manitoba, Ontario, Quebec. We do the Prairies and western Canada. We used to do Maritimes, but we dropped that one."

Paonessa's particularly fond of Quebec. "We've opened up a Painters of Quebec series. I've been looking for Quebec artists. I've been able to find a few through galleries." Marketing staff pens the sentiments. Greeting cards contain *sentiments* — don't call them verses, don't call them poems. "I usually do some type of proofreading. If there's a mistake. I try to make sure the sentiments are simple. Sometimes it just says 'Season's Greetings.' That's all you need."

Merry Christmas from
McCORMACK MOTORS

☐ DECEMBER ☐

	1	2	3	4	5	6
7	8	9	10	11	12	13
14	15	16	17	18	19	20
21	22	23	24	25	26	27
28	29	30	31			

23

WALL CALENDARS

MERRY CHRISTMAS! SAYS my calendar. *Merry Christmas from McCormack Motors!* My grandparents ran McCormack Motors, a dealership and garage. Dad worked there in his teens. *In the heart of Apsley, Ontario!*

Come Christmas, my grandparents thanked customers with calendars. On mine: a painting. A clapboard church. Snow on the steeple. It hangs over my desk. I have it open to December 1957. Christmas was a Wednesday.

Circa Confederation, wall calendars were new. Almanacs and diaries had been the common means of marking time. Office calendars, that's what they were called. "Messrs. Fisher & Co. have just issued an official calendar and Postal Guide," reported the Montreal *Gazette* in December 1875, "being a large card and adopted for hanging up in offices and counting rooms."

Companies gave away calendars for free. Calendars consisted of cards with page-a-day pads glued on. Few cards had pictures; most had words. The Railway and Newspaper Advertising calendar had advertising rates. The Standard Life Insurance calendar had insurance rates.

People preferred pictures. Calendars dropped text, added woodcuts or engravings. The *Manitoba Daily Free Press* published an advertising calendar, then published a review: "A more convenient calendar for office use could not have been devised." The calendar featured a lino-cut of the *Free Press* building. "It is entirely a home production, and perhaps the first calendar entirely manufactured in this Province." The paper mentions a couple of other calendars. They were advertisements as well. A brewery's. A lumber company's. Both had engravings of their buildings. They were not reviewed as kindly as the *Free Press* calendar.

"Adjectives fail. Superlatives are useless," enthused a Montreal stationer describing the prints of Louis Prang. Prang mastered the art of chromolithography in the 1860s. Over the ensuing decade, his Boston-based company manufactured the most colourful Christmas cards and calendars. "Christmas Wishes in Lovely Form" — that's what Prang calendars were, and that's how stationers sold them.

Prang's calendars weren't promotions but *objets*. Pretty. And they cost a pretty penny. People paid up to six dollars for them. "A calendar that is made for the home," as an advertisement put it, "and not for the office!"

A new class of wall calendar, the art calendar, was born. Prang's art calendars came printed with butterflies and robins and angels on high. A Montreal stationer advertised items imported from France — an Eiffel Tower calendar, diamond dust glued to it. Another art calendar printed on snowflake paper. "It glitters like silver and looks," said an ad in 1889, "like interwoven flakes of snow."

From England came literary calendars. "There is a Tennyson calendar," the ad reported, "consisting of a selection from one of the Laureate's poems, with an appropriate picture for each month." Tennyson not to your taste? How about Hawthorne? Schiller? Eliot?

Prang's Victoriana fell from fashion. When it came to art calendars, at the outset of the Great War, a newspaper noted that "the Gibson girl and the college youth encroach where once the angels and Christmas scenes alone held sway."

Charles Dana Gibson was an American illustrator. In 1914, a Copp Clark catalogue page was devoted to "The Gibson Calendar." "Seven new pictures in Pen and Ink style." Among the pictures: "Keep the Mouth Closed," "The Reason Dinner was Late," "Advice to the Mentally Feeble."

Copp Clark sold calendars imported from America. Copp Clark's best-seller was "The Annual Favourite" — the Harrison Fisher calendar. Harrison Fisher illustrated for *Scribner's* and the *Saturday Evening Post*. An American artist famous in Canada, as was James Montgomery Flagg, as was Sarah S. Sitwell. N. C. Wyeth, Winslow Homer — Copp Clark carried them, as well.

Canadian artists? Copp Clark didn't have any in their catalogue.

"Every Canadian Should Have a Copy of 'Historic Days of Canada.'" "Historic Days" was a calendar offered by a Montreal stationer in December of 1897. For every month, there was an illustration of an important scene — a battle being fought, a treaty being signed. "Just the thing to send to friends abroad."

The rarest of things — art calendars that featured Canadian art. They remained rare until the 1930s, when Rous and Mann came out with Canadian Artists calendars, counterparts to their Canadian Artists cards. Though Rous and Mann sold them to stores across the country, they targeted school boards, "by whom their educational and artistic values should be appreciated."

Each calendar boasted twelve different paintings by twelve different artists, Casson, Carmichael, and Lismer among them. At Christmas, Rous and Mann advertised their services by chromolithographing the same pictures onto advertising calendars, which they gave away to good customers. "The three-sided desk calendars," says *DA, A Journal of the Printing Arts*, "soon became a trademark of the company." Rous and Mann soon began to produce them on behalf of other companies.

In the 1900s, Rolph Clark Stone, Ltd., of Toronto were renowned for their chromolithography. Colour lithos, also known as chromos. Promo chromos. That's what Rolph Clark Stone made. Canada's banks, insurance companies, and industries commissioned calendars. Or, as a critic called them, "announcements of great corporations in the guise of works of art."

A. H. Hider was a war artist — Canada's greatest, according to the Canadian War Museum. Hider painted battles from the Boer War. He painted military uniforms. He captured a military parade as it crossed the Plains of Abraham. Critics also acclaimed him as Canada's finest painter of animals. Horses were his specialty. His relatives received horse paintings as gifts. A relative of his once commented, "[It was] just as well, because most could not afford to purchase his work."

Hider never made a living from war painting. He earned his keep as a commercial artist, working for sixty years for Rolph Clark Stone, illustrating advertising calendars. He painted racehorses owned by the Dawes Brewery of Montreal. He painted a logo for the Calgary Brewing and Malting company: a buffalo barrelling across plains. Flour mills for flour mills.

"The Yuletide Giveaway," *Saturday Night* magazine called it. By the 1950s, Canadian companies were producing tens of millions of dollars' worth of advertising calendars. Some calendar companies kept illustrators in house. Some imported art from image banks in the United States. Art, said *Saturday Night*, could be divided into three categories. One was barbershop art: women wearing almost nothing. "Where men are still men — such as in garages, logging camps, and the Dew Line — the girlie calendar reigns supreme. But there's a downright puritanical absence of nudes."

Human-interest art included cherubic children, mothers holding babies, grandfathers fishing with grandsons. Kittens and puppies and stallions — these counted as human interest, too. Scenic art involved landscapes. Summer lakes, woods in winter. The snowy steeple is scenic. Just not in Apsley, there's no steeple there.

"From the kitchen wall to the factory office to the executive desk, the calendar is the time-honoured organization tool . . . and the one gift businesses love to give each holiday season." The quote comes courtesy of the Calendar Advertising Council — the CAC, an offshoot of PPAC, the Promotional Products Association of Canada. The council represents Canadian manufacturers of advertising calendars. In the 1950s, calendars were printed on presses. Today they're printed on presses, on computers, on copiers. "In addition to paper," says the CAC, "calendars are manufactured on cloth, plastic, metal, wood, glass and other materials."

Illustrations are out. The bulk of contemporary advertising calendars feature photographs. Art styles remain the same — scenic art: shots of Rockies, of Prairie grain, of Atlantic lighthouses. DWB, a promotional-products firm in Ontario, sells a golf course calendar. It's scenic, to some. DWB also sells kitten calendars. It does not sell girlie calendars.

"Part of the beauty of a calendar is its time value," says the CAC. "As the previous year's calendar becomes obsolete, it's replaced with a new one — and a new advertising message. Recipients actually look forward to a new calendar each year from a business they patronize. It becomes a tradition."

Who keeps old calendars? My grandparents didn't keep any. I found mine at a flea market. I paid a steep price. Was it worth it? I contact the Calendar Collectors Society, an American organization with an international membership. The answer is yes and no.

"Calendars with local advertising, naturally, bring the most money in that particular area," the society says. My calendar has sentimental interest. A piece of the past. The most coveted calendars feature art by the stars of illustration. "Some collectors build entire collections around calendar art . . . produced by famous artists," the society says. Tony Sarg. Norman Rockwell. An old Maxfield Parrish can bring hundreds of dollars at auction.

Celebrity calendars command high prices. The Dionne Quintuplets shilled for scores of companies, who used their pictures to push products. Every year came another installment: Quints in pink dresses, 1937. Quints in springtime, 1942. Quints on the seashore, 1943. The seashore in North Bay?

"Age is only one determining factor in estimating value," the society says. Contemporary advertising calendars are collectible. If they're what the Calendar Collector Society calls "companion collectibles," calendars issued by Coca-Cola, McDonald's, John Deere, "or hundreds of other corporations" whose ephemera collectors covet.

Contemporary collectibles fit "into a sports collection, celebrity collection, or political or any number of other collections." NHL calendars for hockey collections. In Canada, Royal paraphernalia's prized — calendars commemorating the wedding of Charles and Diana, the death of Diana, the twentieth century's five coronations. *Coronation Street*.

"The calendar collecting area can take various forms," says the Calendar Collectors Society. Besides advertising calendars, there are art calendars. Besides art calendars, there are perpetual calendars, desk calendars, pocket calendars, postcard calendars, novelty calendars, calendar plates, and calendar towels.

Advent calendars? I don't know anyone who collects them. It's too difficult. Turn-of-the-century calendars are in museums. Few were manufactured. Few survived the season. Kids drew on them. Snow rusted.

24

ADVENT CALENDARS

WIBBELE. A GERMAN word that means "little candy." In nineteenth-century Germany, parents glued *Wibbeles* to paper. Children ate a candy on every day of Advent — a candy and a gob of glue.

The earliest Advent calendars were homemade. In some homes, kids drew with chalk on doors — a line per day during December. Some parents cut out pictures and kids tacked them to a wall, a picture a day, making a religious scene.

In the early 1900s, German stores started selling commercial Advent calendars. The calendars weren't candied, they were chromolithographs. Professionally printed, they featured Bible scenes — Noah's Ark was popular. Windows opened onto pictures of angels, cherubs.

Some windows opened onto religious mottoes. Pictures proved more popular.

After 1910, Advent calendars started to appear in countries across Europe. As one Advent calendar company put it, "the Advent Calendar started a triumphal way around the globe."

World War II killed the Advent calendar. Wounded it, anyway. The German government rationed cardboard, prohibited the production of illustrated calendars. Then came Richard Sellmer, a German entrepreneur. In 1946, he ventured into Stuttgart's U.S. Military Zone and purchased paper. The Americans issued him a licence to print.

Sellmer set up an assembly line in his living room, working by hand. He called his first Advent calendar "Little Town." It was a triptych — a main page with fold-out wings — that stood up on its own. It depicted a typical little town in the Black Forest. Before the bombings. Americans snapped them up.

Sellmers still make Advent calendars. "The company is not large," Frank Sellmer says of Richard Sellmer Verlag, the family firm, with a staff of ten occupying 500 square metres in Stuttgart. "We have a large output," he says. They keep a million or so calendars on hand.

Richard Sellmer's son Tim now runs Richard Sellmer Verlag. Tim's son Frank is second-in-command. Frank Sellmer started in the family business when he was thirteen years old. "Our ten-week-old son is also in the company day by day," he jokes. Frank Sellmer sells designs his grandfather sold. "Little Town" remains a mainstay, but the company adds new designs yearly.

"We have several freelance artists," Frank Sellmer says. "We give them a theme, they make a sketch, and we discuss it." Artists design cover art, back pictures, the cutting outline.

"In the past, I got the real paintings, but today nearly all artists supply us with digital files." The artwork is then printed by a professional printing company, and shipped to headquarters, where Richard Sellmer Verlag's workers die-cut windows in the covers. "The die-cut machinery is actually a printing machine which we use for cutting," Frank Sellmer says. "It's important that if you open the window, the back picture fits."

Sellmer asks that Santa Claus appear behind the sixth window of each calendar, and that a Nativity scene appear behind the twenty-fourth. Other than that, there's no rhyme or reason to where the hidden pictures appear. Workers spray glue on the covers. A belt carries the covers under a waterfall of glitter. Glitter used to be made from metal. Now it's plastic. "The glitter machinery is an invention by my father," Frank Sellmer explains. "As it is unique machinery, we do not publish detailed pictures of it. It's a secret."

Richard Sellmer Verlag also makes advertising Advent calendars. It custom-made a calendar for *Reader's Digest* magazine. A Hollywood studio hoped a calendar would help promote *Bingo*, a movie about Santa's magical dog. "We do many bespoke productions but have never produced one for a Canadian customer. Unfortunately."